A VICTORIAN FARMER'S DIARY

A VICTORIAN FARMER'S DIARY

WILLIAM HODKIN'S DIARY 1864-66

LIFE IN AND AROUND BEELEY ON THE CHATSWORTH ESTATE

Edited by

T. A. Burdekin

Derbyshire County Council
Cultural & Community Services Department
2003

Published by:
Derbyshire County Council
Cultural & Community Services Department

ISBN 0 903463 72 5

British Library in Cataloguing in Publication Data:
a catalogue record for this book is available from the British Library.

Front cover:
Norman House Farm, Beeley.
From a painting by William Hodkin's granddaughter.

Produced for Derbyshire County Council Cultural & Community Services Department by
Country Books, Courtyard Cottage, Little Longstone, Bakewell, Derbyshire DE45 1NN
Printed and bound in England

CONTENTS

Nostalgia affects us all and it plays a large part in our interest in the land and the lives of those who lived and worked it nearly 150 years ago.

To us at Chatsworth the Hodkin family were near neighbours and the diary of day-to-day life of the tenant of one of the many small farms in the village of Beeley is a fascinating document.

It brings home to us the physical hardships taken for granted, the number of men and women working small acreages with no machinery, the importance of each animal, the disaster of a natural death, but the almost daily occupation of William Hodkin of killing pigs and sheep for other people as well as for his own family, the Fair and Feast days, the row with the parson (forgiven after an apology from the reverend gentleman), returning home to Beeley from Bakewell by train, disagreements with the Chatsworth agent, and, best of all, the short sharp description of the birth of a daughter is recorded like the birth of a calf, with no emotion. *"The Mrs very poorly all day she was delivered of a little girl at 45 minutes after 3pm."* This news was buried in the humdrum work of the day *"I went to Edensor and Pilsley took some flour, I took the young black horse went forward to Bakewell Market. Paid Mr Jepson for 3 qrs of malt, paid my subscription to the Bakewell Farmers Club. I ordered 3 qrs more malt of Mr Jepson at 56s. per qr."*

Mr Hodkin's handwriting must have been a big challenge to his great grandson, but thanks to Mr Alec Burdekin's persistence we have a vivid picture of the life and work of one of hundreds of thousands of"small" farmers in this country who, lest we forget, made our loved landscape what it is today. The diary is a great contribution to the history of this neighbourhood, but is also certain to be of interest to those from further afield.

WILLIAM HODKIN 1830-1899

My Great Grandfather William Hodkin wrote a diary in 1864, and though I had known of its existence, it wasn't until April this year that it came into my possession following the death of my sister last year. There had been at least two other volumes in the family, but this one is the only one known to have survived.

So it was with some excitement that I opened it and began to read, or at least tried to read. Though in remarkable condition for its age, the style of writing, the unusual spelling and lack of punctuation made it difficult to follow. So I set myself the task of transcribing it into a readable format.

I have left most of the original spelling, added punctuation only where necessary and tried to present it as it was written.

The diary gives a picture of life on a small Derbyshire farm on the Chatsworth Estate, the day-to-day work, and the people involved in life in the village of Beeley. Frustratingly, it includes little of the life and work of his wife, only mentioning her occasionally, although by 1864 she had four sons, and a daughter was born the following year. No mention is made of who did the milking, butter or cheese making or brewing, one suspects it was the job of Mrs Hodkin and her servant girls who appear on the Census for 1871.

Great Grandfather William was as much a dealer as farmer, buying and selling a variety of goods such as coal, wool and flour. The prices are extremely interesting, and would appear to show agriculture in a very strong financial state, and yet I have a letter, signed by forty six of the farming tenants on the Estate in November 1885,only twenty years later, requesting a reduction in rent, "Due to the depressed state of agriculture". As far as I can ascertain, £1 in 1866 would be worth £43 today. It is also a period of rapid change, the coming of the railways had made travel and the movement of goods very much easier, though he does have to rely on the stage coach to reach certain areas, or walk.

There are words, which I have found impossible to decipher, and certain terminology and phrases, which are new to me. Maybe someone will be able to fill in the blanks for me. As an example, on May 5th 1864, and other dates, William refers to 'draising manure', a term for which I have been unable to find a meaning, I have had suggestions, but I await confirmation, Strangely enough, he doesn't use the term in subsequent years.

I have received help from The Derbyshire Libraries and Heritage Department, The Chatsworth Estate and numerous individuals, particularly, Mr & Mrs C. Noble who now reside at Norman House, Beeley, William Hodkin's old home, and encouragement and interest from many people, too many to mention individually.

I wish to acknowledge the use of the report of The Great Review in Chatsworth Park, taken from the Derbyshire Times of June 1865, the quote from the 7th Duke's Diary of the same Review, also the map of the Beeley area reproduced from the 1879 Ordnance Survey map with kind permission of the Ordnance Survey.

This has been a fascinating exercise for me, I feel I have begun to know someone from my family who was before my time. I regret that this appears to be the only volume to have survived. Perhaps there are more in some archives somewhere!

T. A. Burdekin,
Cornwall. August 2002.

GLOSSARY OF TERMS USED

Annetto	Annatto, (Bixaceae) A vegetable colouring used in the making of butter and cheese
Cross cutting the fallow.	Ploughing crosswise already ploughed ground.
Hefted the Hoggs	Put male lambs out to graze.
Hamburgh	Hamburg cock, a breed of poultry
Oregons	Probably a breed of poultry,
Belted the ewes	Removed soiled and dirty wool before lambing.
Washing the beltings	Washing the dirty wool.
Kildrkin of pork dubbin	Kilderkin, a cask or container of 18 gallons.
Cow Club	An Insurance scheme, mainly for the cottager. At the time, a subscription of 2 shilling per quarter, per cow.
Draising Manure	Either dropping in heaps or spreading manure
Ringing the pigs	Putting a ring in the pig's nose to prevent rooting the soil.
SS & SSS & XXX Flour	Grades of flour.
Fourths, Bran Sharps	Known as offals, after the fine flour is removed.
Cutting Oats	Probably with a scythe and tied in sheaves by hand.
Shearing Wheat	The same, but why the different term?
Winnowing	Putting the oats through a machine to remove the chaff after threshing.
Adgistment	Renting grazing for sheep or cattle.
Nocking Manure	Knocking out the lumps left after spreading.
Swingletrees	Devices to attach the horses to an implement.
Shot the Oats	Emptied the sack of oats into a heap.
Strike of Grains	A measure of quantity not weight
Riding the walls	Probably cutting the grass & brambles around the field.
Pitching the yard	Laying a new stone yard surface.
Setting the Pales	Slabs of stone set on end to form a fence.
Seaton the calves	Probably an early form of vaccination
Calf with Speed	Probably a local term for "Blackleg" A fatal disease.
Calf with gir	Almost certainly scouring, a fatal condition then
A soughf	A drain for water.

A list of Fairs, Feasts, Shows and Wakes mentioned in William Hodkin's diary 1864–66. Plus one or two business trips further afield.

1864
May
4th Weds.	Chesterfield Fair.
16th Mon.	Bakewell Fair.
24th-26th Tues.-Thurs.	Ashford Feast [also called Wakes]

June
23rd-24th Thurs.-Fri.	Buxton Well Dressing

July
3rd Sunday	Beeley Wakes.
17th Sunday	Holmesfield Feast.

August
3rd to 8th Weds.-Mon.	To the Isle of Man via Manchester and Liverpool.
14th Sun.	Baslow Feast.
26th Friday	Bakewell Fair.

September
16th Friday	Cattle Show at Derby.
26th Monday	Chesterfield Fair.

October
6th Thurs.	Cattle Show at Bakewell.
12th Weds.	To Manchester, for a tea with the Wesleyans.
15th-17th	To Liverpool/
24th Sat.	Matlock Fair.

November
14th Mon.	Bakewell Fair Market.
25th.Friday.	Chesterfield Fair.

1865.
January
26th. Thursday.	Horse Fair at Chesterfield.

April
17th Mon.	Bakewell Fair Market.

June
5th Mon.	Winster Fair.
11th-12th Sun. Mon.	Ashford Feast.
17th Sat.	Beeley Club Feast.
24th Tues.	Matlock Fair.
30th Mon.	Newhaven Fair.

July
9th Sun.	Beeley Feast.
16th Sun.	Holmesfield Feast.

August.
9th Weds.	Baslow Feast and Concert

October

4th Weds.	Bakewell Cattle Show.
13th Fri.	Hathersage fair.

1865
October

16th Mon.	Bakewell Fair.
24th Tues.	Matlock Fair.
30th Mon.	Newhaven Fair.

1866
January

27th. Sat.	Chesterfield Fair
February	
28th Weds.	Chesterfield Fair.
April	
7th. Sat.	Chesterfield Fair.

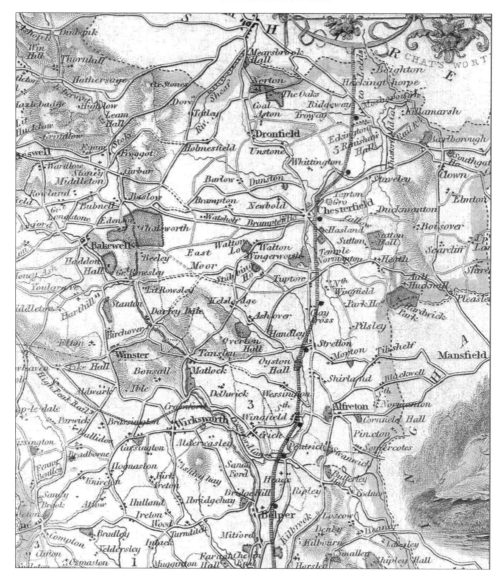

Map showing some of the locations referred to in the diary.
Taken from a map of 1830

THE VILLAGE OF BEELEY

Then and Now

It would be hard to find a better example of the changes that have taken place in rural Britain in the last fifty years than the small village of Beeley on the Chatsworth Estate, Derbyshire. To compare Beeley today with the village of 138 years ago is like looking at different worlds, so great have been the changes.

At the time my Great Grandfather, William Hodkin, wrote his diary in 1864-66 Beeley had much in common with many villages in Derbyshire, it was very self-contained and home to a wide range of occupations. It had a school, resident Rector, shops, blacksmith, a carpenter-builder and, to provide continuity, the Duke of Devonshire as Landlord of most of the properties.

The only known photograph of William Hodkin taken in his old age
© T. A. Burdekin

Whilst the Duke was very much respected, his Agent was more a man to be feared and carried a great deal of authority. Many were the clashes between him and William Hodkin, who thought nothing of going over his head, and referring straight to the Duke, which didn't necessarily make him popular with the Agent.

Until the great changes in agriculture which took place in the mid-20th century, there were eight or nine farms or smallholdings actually in the village. Most had a cow or two, which would be housed near to the house during the winter, and in summer would

15

Edensor church at milking time
© Derbyshire County Council

be taken to graze in Chatsworth Park. The owner would have to travel twice daily to the Park to milk the cows in the open and by hand, and then carry the milk back to the village. Only a few farmers like my grandfather and later his son, my Uncle Bert, had land close enough to home to bring the cows back to the farm for milking. Having 100 acres they would be classed as large farmers!

The Census of 1871 shows that the "Township of Beeley", not just the village, had a total population of 356 and 21 occupations, the majority involved with agriculture or directly employed by the Chatsworth Estate. The current population of the village is a mere 180 people. The school closed in the 1960s and the last shop and Post Office ceased trading in 1990. The Methodist Chapel was built in 1807 and rebuilt and enlarged in1890. Although William Hodkin was a Churchwarden at the village Church, he was one of the donors of £25 towards the costs. The Duke of Devonshire donated the extra land required for the enlarged building. The Chapel was closed in 1996 and was sold to become a private dwelling. Although still very much an estate village, Beeley now has more the appearance of a dormitory or retirement village than the hive of activity it once was.

It is not surprising that many of the villagers were born in the village or were from the nearby area, but it is also remarkable that many came from a

Extract from the 1871 Census Enumerator's Returns showing the Hodkin family

considerable distance, presumably to work at Chatsworth. A shepherd's wife came from Belfast, and a gamekeeper from Middlesex. In 1871 there were 93 children under 14, and large families were common; no wonder the school was active. Entertainments were home produced, with the village Wakes and Fairs or Feasts occurring throughout the year.

The 1871 Census provides us with an interesting list of occupations in Beeley, 21 farmers, the largest farming 175 acres, the smallest with only 7 acres, and employing a total labour force of 28. Chatsworth appears to employ the greatest number, with 37 listed as gardeners, gamekeeepers and general servants. There were also 15 quarrymen and masons, a puddler and a cordwainer, a butcher, an innkeeper, a laundress and 3 seamstresses.

Reading the diary, it is remarkable for us now, to realise the distances which had to be walked just to visit Bakewell for example. Although the arrival of the railways had made travel to places further afield much easier, it would be necessary to walk to the station at Rowsley, walk again from Bakewell station which is some distance from the town centre, and repeat it on the return journey.

I have found it fascinating to visit William Hodkin's home in Beeley, Norman House, which, whilst no longer a farm, is still very much as he would have known it. The dairy with the stone cheese presses outside he would recognise without difficulty, and the stone paving which he describes toward the end of the

Norman House, Beeley, July 2002
The house from the garden
© T. A. Burdekin

Norman House, Beeley, July 2002
The court yard
© T. A. Burdekin

Norman House, Beeley, April 2002. From the village street. Court door mentioned in the diary
© T. A. Burdekin

Norman House, Beeley, July 2002. House and buildings, now dwellings
© T. A. Burdekin

Norman House, Beeley, July 2002. The dairy with cheese presses and grindstone
© T. A. Burdekin

diary is still there. In the Orchard are possibly some of the fruit trees he planted, and the goose pens which he built. Later in his life he moved to Bridge Farm at the entrance to Chatsworth Park, and his son George, my grandfather, took over the tenancy at Norman House and later on, worked the corn mill in the Park. I recall a visit there in the early 1930's when it was still a working mill.

Studies of the Ordnance Survey map of Beeley show the field boundaries are still very much as they were in 1865, and it is possible to put the field names used to most of the fields mentioned in the diary. Being now in the Peak District National Park and a conservation area, it is to be hoped that these vital parts of the landscape will remain untouched however inconvenient they may be to farm.

Characters and folklore seem to go together in rural villages, throughout the country, not just in Derbyshire. Beeley too had its share, and one story concerns a relative on my father's side who lived at Moor Farm, Beeley, a smallholding just below the Chesterfield Road on the outskirts of the village.

Samuel and Hannah Grafton had eleven daughters, who worked on the farm and in his business as quarry owner and stone merchant, but he really hoped for a son to whom he could pass on the business. In May 1843 Hannah was due to give birth to her thirteenth child, one daughter having died in infancy. Hannah had never had much trouble giving birth, but she was now forty two years old and worn out after twenty seven years of regular child bearing. The village mid-wife realised that a doctor was going to be needed, and sent Samuel to fetch one

20

from Chesterfield. He was a good horseman, and normally the journey would have been no trial to him. This time, however, the weather was atrocious, the rain lashed down, and the wind was gale force over Beeley Moor. When Samuel reached the doctor's, he was reluctant to turn out on such a terrible night. Now Samuel was a man of enormous stature, and the doctor was rather puny, also Samuel had a very short temper. Instead of arguing, he picked up the little man and placing him on the horse's back, gave the horse a slap, and sent it off into the night, knowing the animal wouldn't stop until it reached Moor Farm.

Samuel then set off towards home on foot, the roads over the moor were only rough tracks and footpaths in those days. Struggling on through the wild dark weather, Samuel suddenly realised he was lost. He blundered about, knee deep in sodden heather for what seemed like hours. At last, the rain eased a little and Samuel saw a light ahead of him. What happened next, you can judge for yourself, but my father's family always reckoned that Samuel believed the Devil appeared to him. Apparently, they had a long chat, and the Devil agreed that if Samuel gave him his soul he would arrange for the new baby to be a boy. Next thing, Samuel found himself following the light across the moor, and after a short while, found himself back in his own farmyard, to be greeted by his daughters with the news that at last, he had a son!

The story doesn't end there, for, as so often happens, the son did inherit the business and the money that the daughters had worked so hard to make, and he soon made short work of spending it.

I am grateful to a cousin, Mrs Pauline Harrison, a great-great-grand-daughter of Samuel, for this story about Samuel Grafton, one of the characters of Beeley.

THREE-HORSE EQUALIZING WHIPPLETREES.

These are designed for working Double-furrow Ploughs with three horses abreast, so that the draught is equal for each horse, and the ploughman can manage them without a driver.

Price No. 1, for Light Horses £1 10 0 *1.12.6*
,,   ,, 2, for Heavy Horses 1 10 6 *1.15.0*

SLEEP'S PATENT "U" SECTION STEEL WHIPPLETREES.

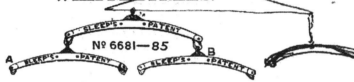

Scientific in Principle, Novel in Design, and Moderate in Price.

NOTE.—The " **U** " Section of Steel, as applied in the Whips, is Patented.

Being made of Wrought Steel Plates bent into **U** shape, these Whippletrees are very strong and rigid, and yet exceedingly light.

Price of 2-Horse Set (as shown above) 17s. 6d. *18.6*
Price when fitted for Three Horses, for working two
in the Furrow and one on the Land 19s. *1.0.0*

WOOD WHIPPLETREES.

These are made of tough English Ash, and are suitable for pair of horses.

Price   ...   .   14s.

"Went to Rowsley with 2 swingletrees to be ironed. 5 December 1864."

APRIL-OCTOBER 1864

Throughout the diary William refers to "Father"— he is actually his Father in law. As an ambitious young man seeking to become a farmer, William did what many young men did and still do, married a farmer's only daughter and so inherited the business.

He was a man of limited formal education but very clever with figures. My Mother, his granddaughter, related how he could add up a column of pounds, shillings and pence, all three columns at once.

He uses a variety of spellings for the same word, variously, Lydgate, Lidget, Hiring gate, Hiring gath, etc., sometimes with a capital letter, often without. Note too his unusual spelling of "Wedensday", which I have left throughout the diary.

His two eldest boys are mentioned, Henry and George, 7 and 5 respectively at the time this was written, and although young, they are expected to do jobs around the farm.

Whilst much of the work is done by hand, he does have a barn thrashing machine, powered by a horse walking round the horse gin.

Coal is fetched from Boythorpe Colliery, near Chesterfield, though later in the diary, increasingly, coal comes to Rowsley station, shortening the journey for the horse and cart. Flour also comes to Rowsley, mainly from Newark, but he still uses the local water powered mills at Edensor and Baslow for grinding Indian Corn, (Maize) and oats.

Mr Shenton is the vet from Bakewell, Mr Worrrall, the Chatsworth Farm Manager.

The Vicar of Beeley is the Revd. Outram soon to retire and be replaced by Revd. Sculthorpe with whom he has a disagreement, although we don't know the full details. Mr Cottingham is the Chatsworth Agent, a man of some position in the area. Other names are of his neighbours in the village and surrounding area.

A barn thrashing machine powered by a horse gin
© Museum of English Rural Life, University of Reading

DIARY BELONGING TO WILLIAM HODKIN

1864

April 16.	Went to Chesterfield Market with the light cart had the horse down in going down [C]cathole did not hurt him much, Sold 2 qrs of hay seeds to Mr Mason at 7s per qr. Bought of Mr Mason 5 stone of Red clover seed and one stone of Treafoil and 6 strike of Italian rye grass to sow in the South field. Father in law looking after cattle. John Smith began cross cutting fallow, W Ludlam cleaning shed and cowhouse out at Lydgath, Mr Sam Albert poorly. Mr Wrench attending him, John Downs fetched one hamburgh cock for Saml Downs price 2s, a good growing day.
April 17th. Sunday.	Albert not much better.
April 18th.	Went to Bakewell Market. Bought one cow of Mr Howard of Hartington Moor for 14£ warranted alright. Bought of Robert Evans of Beeley 4 pigs, 1£ 4s 6d each, received of Mr Ford of Sheldon 4£ 18s for 3¹/₂ qrs of Poland oats, Paid Mr Else of Darley Mill on A/c 16£ 4s Father went to Bakewell, John Smith took ¹/₂ ton of coal to the Beeley Moor coal pit, looked after cattle and went rowling the oats in the afternoon, day fine, Albert a little better.
Tuesday. April 19th.	Put 8 goslings to their Mother. Went on Beeley Moor went down in the Coal Pit came home and gardened a little then went and hetted the hoggs into the Morton Greave Father looked after the cattle and gardened a little. John rowling a little and then cross cutting the day out.
	The cow calved that I bought yesterday, bull calf.
Wedensday 20th.	Went to Harwood in the morning bought one cow to calve

in the course of the week. Mrs Drabble to keep the cow untill she hath calved and she to have the calf 15£ is the price. Went to Bakewell and paid the income tax and walked back over calton and loaded 2 loads of hay at calton houses John and Thomas Downs met me with the carts, came home and we settled with each other I paid him for 8qrs of oats that I had in February. John ploughing fallow in the morning Father looking after the cattle &e.

Thursday 21st. Choping for the cows and horses in the morning, went to the coal pit before noon, Afternoon jobing about, sold John Oxspring one bull calf for 7s. sold Cawdwell of Winster one bull calf 37s. and one fat cow for 19£, and ten shillings returned, to be be delivered on Monday May the 2nd. John Smith finished ploughing the first time. W Ludlam thrashing till noon, afternoon gathering stones in bull hawk. Father looking after cattle &e. I went to Edensor at night took Mr Spencer some flour & Mr Milner 1/2 cwt. Bran, very hot dry weather for the last 4 days Mr Evans of Allport sent me 3 loads of oatmeal at 27s 6p per load.

Friday 22nd. Jobing about house in the morning then went and sowed two acres of ryegrass in south field before noon. Went to Bakewell in the afternoon and did not arrive home untill 9 o'clock at night rode with Mr Lees there and back. John breaking down the fallow Mr Ludlam gathering stones in the cowley Lydgate Father looking after cattle &e. Thomas Froggatt came and paid for all he owed up to this date. Cut S Ludlam 5 stones of oatmeal. Made the Oregons up to keep them out of peoples gardens.

Saturday 23rd. Went to the sheep, brought one lamb home and killed it it was not very well. Put another kade lamb to the ewe and she appears to take to it. Went into the South field sowing clover seed, sowed about 4 acres and sowed 2 of it with rye grass. John Smith went to Stoney Middleton for lime for the hiring gate with one horse, The other horse W Ludlam Rowling the fallow and harrowed part of it Rowling in the afternoon in the south field when I had sown the small seeds, one lamb died belonging to an hogg one sheep lambed, not sure wether there is another to lamb or not. Father looking after the cattle fine hot day and fine frosty night.

Sunday 24th. Thomson of Darley came and paid for one sack of flour 1£ 15s. Mr Stockdale from Baslow preached at our church in the afternoon.

Monday 25th. Ground 1/2. Load of malt for Mr Hall of Edensor took Buckley one sack of flour and finished sowing small seeds in south field. Father helping me and looking after cattle. I went to Gladwins Mark at night Recd. an account of John Hutchinson 1£ due to me 1£ 1s. from there I went to Harwood, Paid 15£ for one cow and brought her home, bought her very dear Mr Tomlinson of Baslow sent 4£ 10s for half a ton of cake. Mr Travis called at night to see us. John rowling and harrowing in the fallow in the afternoon. Finished rowling the south field let John have 12s when going to Bakewell. Shenton called and brought powders for the filly And looked at the old

Off milking in the fields
© Derbyshire County Council

cows feet and ordered us to poultice it and promised to call again tomorrow. Henry went with me for the cow to Gladwins Mark and Harwood.

Tuesday 26th.

Morning to John Hawksworth 1 sack of flour and many little jobs about home. Afternoon cut the lambs and cut the ewe lambs tails and belted the ewes. Began ploughing the potato ground second time over John rowling in the morning, after dinner gathering the rubbish off the fallow. Father looking after the cattle and assisting me with the sheep and gathering the twitch off the fallow. Brewing the third time for the harvest, W Norman paid Matthew Halkworth Bill 15£. A fine day but rather cold, rather like for rain Rain would do a deal of good.

Wedensday 27th.

Looked up and sent off to Newark 43 sacks. Killed 2 pigs to go to Chesterfield tomorrow. Went to Calton Houses for the remainder of a stack of hay that I had bought of Mr Trikers. Sent Mr Jepson 3 of his sacks. Mr Ludlam sent 8 sacks home that I lent him and 2 that he did not bring back, took Mr Ludlam 1 sack of flour. John ploughing in tho morning, afternoon he and Thomas Downs went with me for hay with two carts. Father looking after cattle and assisting me some times and got part of one potato pit in, a dry cold North East wind

Thursday 28th.

Took two pigs to Chesterfield to George Crofts Pork

Butcher, 18 stones 1lb. At 6s. 4d. per stone, 5£ 14s 5¹/2d. bought a leg of pork of him,17¹/2lb at 7¹/2d per pound 9s 8d. got home about 3 oclock Went to Calton Lees and measured a haystack belonging to Mr Travis, about a 100 yards in it offered him 35£ for it but he refused it he wanted 40£. Got home about half past 12 o'clock at night. John finished ploughing the potato ground and harrowed it and rowled and harrowed it again. Father looking after the cattle and George Ludlam was intered this day at Beeley aged 38 years, another dry cold day North East wind.

Friday 29th.

I went with John in the fallow all day spread the lime on the potato ground father looking after cattle and finished getting potato put in. Recd. of Sarah Stone 1£ 10s. left on 3s. and rather a cold day barometer lowering wind changing South west and North rather likely for some rain.

Saturday 30th.

Went into the fallow came home and gardened untill noon sowed onions and lettuce and carrotts and radish and mustard and cress and made ground ready for cauliflower. Went to Calton houses in the afternoon with John and two horses and a wagon for a load of wood. John went to Stoney Middleton for lime in the morning and took it in the hiring gate. Thomas Downs Rowling and harrowing the potato ground and carrying water to slack the lime and gathering twitch. Father looking after the cattle and gardening sowed two rows of peas another dry cold day wind changing barometer rising a little drawed four sheep barren for Bakewell market on Monday.

Sunday 1st. May.

A very fine warm morning began to rain a little toward night

Monday 2nd.

Went to Bakewell market with 4 barren sheep Sold them to Mr Tomlinson of Rowsley at 50s. each took one red stirk also and sold it to Mr Gardon of Bakewell for 7£ she Kast a dead calf and was rather poor. John Grindey went with me Paid Mr Orme for one Kildrkin? pork dubbin 1£ 7s. Paid Mr Bowman for two cwt. Cake 19s. Father looked after the cattle and then went to Bakewell market. John ploughing the fallow Mr G Holmes had one stirk with her womb down I went and tried to put it back but could not Shenton came and put it back and the cow is doing well a very fine growing day Some nice rain Cawdwell fetched the fat cow the old one.

Tuesday 3rd.

Went with John into the fallow finished ploughing it John spread some lime and harrowed it. Fetched 20 sacks of flour &10cwt. of bran and 20cwt. of sharps From Rowsley

28

station that I had from Messrs Thorpe & Co of Newark. Went to the quarterly meeting of the cow club at night and have paid 16s. the quarterly subscription, also paid Mr Outrams subscription 2s Father looking after the cattle & spreading manure at the Lydgate a very fine growing day some rain in the morning barometer rising a little.

Wedensday 4th.

I went to Chesterfield Fair tried to sell a horse 4 years old called Short but did not sell him Bought 7 pigs at 22s. each made it late before I was home Mr Buckley was with me John draising some manure and began Rowling Cow Close Father looking after cattle & etc a very fine growing day began to rain about noon.

Thursday 5th.

Went and draised some manure in the Bull balk and cow close then came home and was weighing flour and took some out Looked all the sheep over and cleaned all that wanted it. Took the hoggs into the far common field and the ewes and lambs into the farmstead and the Cowley Lydgate Went to Edensor and Pilsley at night with flour and sold Matthew Grindley 2 pigs at 25s. each and George Holmes 1 at 25s. and S Gardner 1 that I bought of R Evans at 31s.. John finished Rowling bull balk and Cow Close Father looking after cattle & gathering stones a very fine growing day thunder and rain at night .

Friday 6th.

Went to the Lydgate draising manure in the Cowley Lydgate and the great Lydgate Planted some cawleyflower plants Went to the Hill Top at night to fetch the Mrs Home. John went to Boythorpe collery for coal for ourselves. Thomas Downs spreading manure in the great lydgate and rowling a little in the afternoon and only came home at noon. A very fine day, growing day rained heavy at night.

Saturday 7th.

Went with Thomas Downs gathering stones in the cowley Lydgate in the morning Thomas finished gathering the cowley Lydgate in the afternoon and gathered a few in the great Lydget. I took the young horse to the Hill Top and left Mr Lees 1/2 bag of flour then went to the Lydgate and Rowled the cowley Lydgate then at night went into the Old Park shooting Jackdaws with Mr Munroe and a few others. John went to Boythorpe for coal for Mr Outram Father looking after cattle and spreading dropings in the Lydget a beautiful fine growing day.

In the Margin Let John have on acct. for wages 1£ 8s.

Sunday 8th.

A fine day colder towards night wind turned into the North East.

Monday 9th.

Looking after cattle went to look at the sheep at night and found one lamb with a leg broken, took it up to Mr Cockers at night and he killed it called at Mr Jepsons and he promised me he would look at it next morning and perhaps buy some of it. Father went to Matlock Fair got home about 4oclock John went to Boythorpe for coal for Mr Spencer of Edensor, a cold north East wind.

Tuesday 10th.

Went with John setting potatoes and Henry went with us and managed to set potatoes very nicely. Father looking after cattle in the morning went with us in the afternoon Thomas Downs went with us also in the afternoon, we set 15 rows in all across the top end at the far side of the Bering Gate. Father planted Kidney Beans at night and one row of Peas. Cousin William Bower came at night got to our house about 1/2 past 8 oclock. A cold day again North East wind. Changed with Wm. Ludlam 11½ stones of flour for 16 stones 3lb of wheat.

Wedensday 11th.

Went to Rowsley Station intending to go to Dove Holes to see Uncle Charles with Cousin W Bower but was one minute to late for the train came home and helped John to gather one load of stone of the fallow. Then went to Rowsley to the Late Mrs Tomlinsons sale bought 4 rush bottomed chairs at 1s 8d each and one pair of shelving for 8d and a lot of cut firewood for 1s 8d one pair of good blanket for 15d and one large deal table with three drawers for 14s. and three rabbit traps at 1s 10d each and a few more sundries. John draging the fallow and harrowing the rest of the day. Thomas Downs thrashing a little in the afternoon and breaking stones for the road to the hiring Gate. Father looking after cattle in the morning went to the sale in the afternoon, another cold day north east wind.

Thursday 12th.

Helped John to load the things that I bought yesterday then went to Dove Holes to see Uncle Charles and found him with a very bad leg. Went to see the ebing and flowing well with cousin Wm. Bower. Returned home by the 8 oclock train at night called and paid 2£ 4s. 10d for the things that I bought yesterday. Sarah Halksworth went to Edensor about the lamb Mr Jepson took one quarter and the remainder she brought home. John and Thomas Downs leading manure on the turnip fallow in the afternoon. Father looking after cattle and gardening a little another cold day north east wind.

Friday 13th.

John and me set a few potatoes in the morning then I went and helped make up the sheep wash and I and Henry Downs washed our sheep 37, and Mr Grafton 25 and S Ludlam 17 and S Downs 6 finished about 5 oclock. John got quite drunk, lent T Froggatt Short to go to Winster for

At the sheep wash
© WH Brighouse

one load of hay. Paid to John Evans for 3 loads of meal 4 £ 10s. Father went to Ashford about the Income Tax, My Mrs went to Bakewell Market in the afternoon, let Mrs Grindey have one quarter of the lamb for 4s. the remainder will use ourselves. A fine warm day but wind still North East Turned out our milk cows to grass in the Morton Greave and pits

Saturday 14th.

Henry went with me with two stirks and one calf on calton to stay for the summer. Thomas Downs and John and Father seting potatoes in the Forenoon and Henry and Father and I finished in the afternoon. John finished harrowing the fallow and broke two loads of stone on the road up Southfield. Father went to Lydget at night with John Holmes to look at a bull calf but they did not bargain bid 3£ 10s for him. I went shooting Rooks and Jackdaws at night with R Evans and Mr Munroe and Mr Swain a very fine sunny day.

Sunday 15th.

A very hot day with North east wind.

Monday 16th.

Went to Bakewell Fair sold Mr Grindley 1 qt. bottle of annetto, And Mr Frost of Sheldon 1 qt. bottle ditto. Ordered one pair of new trousers of Mr Hodgkinson,

Henry got measured for a new suit at Mr Clarks Alfred Lees found the cloth. Went to Hilltop at night. Father went to Bakewell Fair allso took light cart and hacker both horses have got the Influensy John thrashing another hot day with East wind. Paid Mr Orme of Bakewell for annetto 6£ 5s. and 25% off 1 £ 12s 6d.

Note: Annetto, his spelling of a vegetable colouring used in making butter and cheese.

Tuesday 17th.

About home in the morning fencing and mending the gate at the milk Field Sold Mr Tomlinson 2 lambs at 27s.each to go next week John finished thrashing and several sundry jobs Father walling gaps up at the Lydget another very hot day with East wind.

Wedensday 18th.

Fencing in the Morton Greave in the morning Father helping me John leading stone from the Cowley Lydget in the morning. Went to Mr Spencers for two loads of ashes in the afternoon Father went walling to the Lydget in the afternoon another very hot day North wind.

Thursday 19th.

Went collecting bills in, John Elliott of Rowsley paid me Mr Duler paid me ordered 10 sacks of flour of Mr Else of Darley. Went to Matlock and Joseph Kirk paid me went to the Hill top in the afternoon and Mr Lees paid me except the last half bag of flour. John ploughing the turnip fallow Father cleaning the beltings that came of the sheep. Old Shaw buld by the Dukes bull, another hot day thunder and lightning very heavy in the afternoon, wind changed in the South very little rain.

Friday 20th.

Jobing about home in the morning went to Rowsley smithy afternoon went to Bakewell. Father gardening, John cleaning the yard &e Mr Else bought 10 sacks of fine flour Thunder and lightning severe excesive hot day I never recollect such hot weather in May.

Saturday 21st.

Shearing sheep Mr H Lees helping me Father wrapping up the wool, clipped 37 in all, 23 ewes and 14 hoggs John cleaning out the turnip house and the ashes out of the ash place, rather cooler wind in the West.

Sunday 22nd.

A fine day not so hot as it was last week

Monday 23rd.

A day missing.

Tuesday 24th.

Went to Ashford Feast and stopped untill Thursday morning. John harrowing the fallow went to Edensor mill in the afternoon with 2 qrs. of oats Father gardened and looking after the house a dry cold day sharp frost last night.

Wedensday 25th. May.

John Rowling and harrowing the fallow Father mowing nettles and rubbish in the orchard and looking after the house. I put 5s. in the sweep at Mr Wells at Bakewell for the great race at Epsom called the Derby, I drew Blair Atholl and Blair Atholl won the race I have to receive 3£ for my wining ordered one tub of lard of Mr Shirland of Sheffield, another dry day rather cold winds at night.

Thursday 26th. Got home from Ashford Wakes about 10 oclock in the morning then jobing about home, in the afternoon karting sheep Father helping me John Rowling and harrowing fallow another dry day North East wind.

Friday 27th. John went to Stoney Middleton for one load of lime got home about noon set the lime out in heaps in the afternoon. I was looking sacks up and sent 31 of Thorpes & 20 of mine to Newark then fencing a little, went to Edensor in the afternoon to pay the Rent and dined with Mr Worrall & Mr Hall & 9 others Mr Worrall started from Edensor before me but I was at home before nine, I went back with Mrs Worrall to seek the Mr Then came home again then I went with Miss Worrall to Chatsworth and Edensor but did not find him, he was got home before I got to Beeley I got home about ½ past five in the morning Father gathering stones round the cowley and Great Lydgets.

Saturday 28th. Weeding corn in south field and setting lime out in the hering?gate John and our Henry helped me John went to Stoney Middleton with two carts for lime got home about noon. Father cutting thistles in Meek field.Rather cold weather and dry high west wind. Old Shaw buld 2nd. Time by the Dukes bull and our own as well.

Mr Munace sent us 6 Rooks, John Smythe brought us one cask of lard from Booth and Shirley of Sheffield.

Sunday 29th. Another dry day with North wind very cold, Blacknose buld by the Dukes bull.

Monday 30th. Went to Bakewell Market Father went to Bakewell too Recd. 3£ for the sweep at Mr Wells I drew the first horse for the Derby John went to Halksworth at Lees with 1 sack of flour called at the mill and brought meal off 2 qrs of Oats. Another dry day Alfred Milnes came at night.

Tuesday 31st. Jobing about home a little, took the calves into the farmstead and took 3 stirks and the black 2 year old colt into the little brook John Rakeing up manure in the great Lydget another dry day North East wind.

Wedensday 1st. June. A very sharp frost last night made very bad work in the gardens potato tops and kidney beans all cut down 6 degrees of frost. I and Father opening a drain that brings water into the farmstead Went to the coal pit at night went down to the bottom John went to Boythorpe for one ton of

The old method of describing the circumstances surrounding this great turn-out of the London people might be resorted to with little variation in this year of grace 1864. The inevitable costermonger was at the bottom of the social scale, whilst royalty was at the top; and they both managed to get to Epsom amidst a host of fellow travellers of every shade, type and description. The old Downs looked as inviting as ever; it was quite Queen's weather, and the recollection of last year's discomfort only heightened the enjoyment of the day. The moment of electrical excitement approached with a seemingly tardy step—the hands appeared to linger on the surface of the watch—the dense throng seemed held in by one emotion, ruled by one instinct, governed by one ambition, to join heart and soul in the grand contest. The cheering was vast as the horses turned out, the variety of colours glancing in the bright May sun, and the large expanse of humanity surged to and fro as if moved by one and the same impulse. Truly, there is a tide in all the affairs of men; it was at the flood at Epsom, and where it led the pavillions of London probably could inform us. What a start! The jockeys give the rein, and the eyes of thousands follow the struggling straining competitors, and there is a rush to the winning post. The promiscuous yell which greets a winner gives no clue to the popular favour which it enjoys, and consequently when Blair Athol shewed in front, and his number was run up on the signal board, it was impossible to guess how well or how ill he stood in the books of speculators in this particular kind of horse flesh. Nothing succeeds like success, and if Blair Athol had not been a favourite before, he would inevitably have been so by reason of his victory, and will wear his laurels to other scenes, scenes gayer perhaps, further removed from the excessive cockneyism of Epsom, but assuredly to no scenes where there can be a vaster exhibition of national life, the life which makes the individual feel proud of existence, and glory in this very questionable pastime.

Blair Atholl's
Derby win
Derbyshire Times
28 May 1864

coal for ourselves Mr Tomlinson fetched the other lamb that he bought from me Sold Mr Cawdwell 5 lambs at 26s each he took one today the 4 to go this month June he paid for one. Another dry day likely for another frost grass and everything wants rain bad.

Along the margin. My Mrs not well to night.

Thursday 2nd.	Jobing about home Ringing 7 pigs and cleaning pigeon coat and hen roost and John helping me and riddling ashes Father weeding in hiring gate another dry day rain wanted very bad all the grass land burning up.
Friday 3rd.	Went rabbitting in the morning caught 9 rabbitts in the pits went to Bakewell in the afternoon the Mrs went with me Recd. of Wm. Hallam 1 £ on account of John Higinbotham's bill Recd.of the county Court office 1£ 3s 6d the remainder of Joseph Bolney's bill Paid Mr Young of Eve Close 4£ 5s. for ½ ton of linseed cake brought with me about 6cwt. bring the remainder the next time I go to Bakewell. Sent one check for 25£ Messrs Thorpe & Co Newark Mr F Lees lent me 2£ Father weeding in the hiring gate in the morning about home in the afternoon John went to Boythorpe for coal for Mr Outram Another dry day a few drops of rain Very likely to be a dry summer.
Saturday 4th.	Jillett buld by our own bull Fetched the nags out of the Churchyard Put 2 weathers and one tup hog in the Mains with 5 ewes and 4 lambs to 2 ewes out of the mains that the lambs were gone off fat the ewes going with the hogs in the new close 16 ewes and 19 lambs in the common piece. Went up to the coal pit went down into the pit and brought a lump of coal home with me. George and Henry went with me painting a little in the afternoon John and Father weeding corn Another dry day North East wind.
Sunday 5th.	William Milnes came to see us from Ashford a little nice rain but not enough to do much good.
Monday 6th.	Went Rabbitting in the Mains Wm. Lees and S Ludlam and Father went with us caught 41 young rabbitts John weeding in the South field and cutting thistles in the mains the rain that came yesterday is all dried up another very hot day.
Tuesday 7th.	Went with Short to the smithy Helped John to load 3 loads of stone took the stone on the road in the south field Father weeding corn very dry and hot weather.

Along the margin. Drabble buld by our own bull.

Wedensday 8th.	Went to Chatsworth with Mr M Lees intending to see Mr Cottingham but he was not at home. Mr Cawdwell came for one lamb and bid money at the big roan cow he offered

Delivering the milk at Rowsley
© Julie Bunting

20£10s. I offered her at 21£ she buld to calve early December. Went to meet Mr Mayhew at Bakewell station at night got home a little after 12 at night John fetched 2 loads of stone in South field in the morning breaking the stone in the afternoon Father weeding corn another dry hot day I did a little painting in the afternoon.

Thursday 9th. Went to Bakewell in the morning not doing much the day out. John fetched 2 loads of stone from the far common piece in the south field breaking stone the day out Father not doing much Jobing about Another hot day Thunder in the afternoon and a little rain towards night but not enough, Elizabeth brewing.

Friday 10th. Cuting thistles in the mains went and looked at the sheep and went on the moor to the coal pit went down the pit and found the chink so that the water can run off. After dinner went to Bakewell Market and brought the remainder of the half ton of cake John fetched one load of stone and finished breaking the stone on the road in the south field Father finished weeding in the hiring gate another dry day, think the heifer was buld.

Saturday 11th.	Fetched 20 sacks of flour 12 of SS and 8 of SSS and 1 ton of fourths and half a ton of bran from Rowsley Station from Thorpe & C of Newark. After dinner jobing about home after tea went rabbitting caught 17 John finished spreading lime in the hiring gate and draged it after dinner. Father cutting thistles in the little brook Jobing about house after dinner another dry day rather hangs for rain.
Sunday 12th.	Some nice rain began to rain about ¼ before 12 oclock at noon rained until after one oclock another shower about 7 oclock.
Monday 13th.	Went to Bakewell Market Bought one fat pig of Mr Outram for 4£ sold it again same day to Mr Mountney For 4£ 7s. Father went to Bakewell Market. John rowling and harrowing the fallow and gathering stones a nice shower of rain about noon.
Tuesday 14th.	Went to Edensor had an interview with Mr Cottingham about the rabbitts who are very much overrun with them Father and John and I drilling and getting manure on the for turnips. A nice shower of rain at night Rosy buld by our own bull.
Wedensday 15th.	Getting manure on for turnips and sowing turnips John and Father with me barometer very low not much rain.
Thursday 16th.	Finished sowing turnips all of us working at sowing turnips all day a very hot day likely to thunder. Mountney called for the pig that I bought of Mr Outram on Monday Paid me 4£ 7s for it I paid Mr Outram 4£ first.
Friday 17th.	Writing in the morning one letter to Thomas Gammon one to J. G. Cottinham Esq. Complaining of being overrun with rabbits and asked him to assist us in looking for another farm. Went to the little brook for the calves and a young horse and brought them to the lidget Father and Henry with me John Smith flat hoeing potatoes Another dry day.
Saturday 18th.	Went to Chesterfield Market, received a letter from Mr. Walton of Halifax to buy him some wool. Bought Mr Henry Lees at 59s.6d.per tod and two or three other lots. John flat hoeing potatoes Father about home doing several little jobs. Mr R Smith called to see us from Cumberland. A nice shower of rain towards night.
	Note: A tod was used in the wool trade as a measure of weight, 28lbs Present day [2002] price for wool is about 150 pence per kg,.
Sunday 19th.	Mr Smith staying with us untill tomorrow morning a nice shower of rain.

Monday 20th.	Went by Edensor and Pilsley to Ashford buying wools, bought about 20 tod varying in price from 57s to 64s 6d. per tod. Came home by the 8 oclock train at night. John finished flat hoeing the potatoes diging the corner to sow it with rape. Father mowing nettles and rubish in the mains and looking the cattle a dry day.
Tuesday 21st.	Took the Gees[e] to the Lydget and brought 4 of the least lambs back into the mains Father with me wrote a letter in the afternoon to Mr Walton informing him of what wool I bought yesterday. John finished diging the corner out that he began yesterday, a few showers of rain.
Wedensday 22nd.	Went to John Siddalls with my wife and Henry and, paid one years interest for 20£ that I have of theirs got home again about ½ past 9 in the evening there had been a good deal of rain there but not much here only a few showers. John fetching stone for Mr Worrall to the Highways from the brickyard at burchill, Father about home.
Thursday 23rd.	Went by the excursion train to Buxton went to Dove Holes station to have seen Uncle Charles but he was gone to Bury, came back to Buxton to the well dressing came home about 9 o'clock. A deal of rain at Buxton it rained nearly all day, a few nice showers at home. John stone leading for Mr Worrall Father about home all day.
Friday 24th.	Sowing the corner in the hiring gate with rape and jobing about home, went to the Lydget in the afternoon, Killed one goose weighing 10¾ lbs for Mr Mayhew charged 57s. for it John went for stone for the highways with one horse, Father went to Buxton well dressing, Jillett buld second time rather a cold day.
Saturday 25th.	Writing all morning painting in the afternoon John went for stone for the highways, Father cutting thistles in the pits he got some cherrys at night rather cold for the time of year.
Sunday 26th.	Cold day for the time of year.
Monday 27th.	Went to Bakewell Market paid into the Sheffield and Rotherham Bank 2£ 10s. for the 50 shares that I hold in the Beeley main collery, Paid Mr Else of Darley Mill 24£ on account, John leading stone to the highways took Mr Hilbert of Edensor 10 stone flour, took Halksworth 1 bag sharps, I and Father fencing between our mains and Mr Ludlams mains in the morning another dry day with cold wind.
Tuesday 28th.	Painting a little shaking sacks and sundry little jobs. Mr Else sent 20 sacks of flour and 1 tod 7lbs of wool, John

went to Boythorpe for coal for ourselves Father cutting thistles a little rain in the afternoon, cawdwell fetched the remaining 2 lambs that he bought the beginning of this month.

Wedensday 29th. Takeing flour out and painting all day, John fetching stone to the Highways Father not doing much, a few little jobs. Mr Robinson came to look at the bull whe agreed to lend him the bull untill the end of October I bought one pig on Monday gave 7£15s. for it, Thomas Gannon came at night rather cold wind a little rain but sadly short of rain.

Thursday 30th. Helping Frank Slater to mend the Court door, took Boxer to the smithy and got the irons repaired for the door, went with Mr Ludlam at night rabbitting caught 5. John went to Boythorpe for one load of coal for Mr Outram, Mr Jonson came to look at Short but he was gone for coal met him on the road and looked at him I must Mr Johnson on Saturday at Chesterfield and try to bargain for him. Thomas Gannon earthing up potatoes, Father weeding corn a very cold day for the time of year and very dry weather.

Friday 1st July. Helping Frank Slater to repair the Court door and hang it and painted it, John fetching stone for the Highways Thomas cuting thistles Father jobing about. Mr Cawdwell of Winster brought us 31lbs of beef paid for it 19s 4d. a slight shower of rain Mr Achinson sent for the bull calf.

Saturday 2nd. Went to Chesterfield weighed Mr Pinders wool and paid for it, let Mr Hardwick have it paid me 4s. 6d. Saw Mr Johnson tried to sell him Short but he could not bargain he had offered 23£10s. I offered him for 24£. Father jobing about home John leading stone to the Highways Thomas hacking over the bottom headland in the hering gate a good [drop] of nice rain, took the milk cows in the Morton greave at night, I wrote to Mr Walton for him to come and take the wool that I have bought.

Sunday 3rd. Beeley Wakes Aunt and Edwin Milnes came from Ashford and Mother and S Pearson came, a few drops of rain.

Monday 4th. Took Mr Deeley 10 st. flour & Smith 10 st. Bought Mr J Goodwin wool and then got an oat stack in, Thomas and Father helping me, John fetching stone for the Highways. Went to calton houses and bought Elliott wool, Paid John on Act. for wage 2£ 0.0, a dry day rather cold.

Tuesday 5th. Went rabbitting in the morning, making bills out at night Father not doing much Thomas thrashing John carting stone to the highways.

Wedensday 6th. Sent 21 of Thorpes and 32 of my sacks to Newark. Mr

Ferguson came and packed the wool that I had bought sold him our own at 63s per tod, 10 tod 27lb. Left Beeley at 5 oclock and went to Ashford and packed one sheet of wool there, then went to Thornley and round by Longstone and Fernstone lane head looking at wool, bought Mr Mawys. John went to Boythorpe for coal for Mr Spencer, Father helping us pack wool Thomas finishing diggin in the head-land in the hiring gate a fine day.

Thursday 7th.

Went down to Rowsley Station with 4 sheets of wool came home and went by coach from Baslow to Owler Bar went round Holmesfield buying wool bought Mr Purstones at 62s. per tod, Mr Henry Sam Hattersley 59s. Mr Morgans 63s, came back by coach to Edensor. John fetching stone to the Highways Thomas thrashing Father about house another dry day.

'Went by coach from Baslow to Owler Bar'
© Derbyshire County Council

Friday 8th.

Went to Bumperper castle bought Mr Wilsons wool and Mr Darbyshire, went to Bakewell in the afternoon with G Wilson, bought Mr Robinson wool 60s. Mr Smith 64s 6d per tod, Alfred Lees came with me home and stayed all night, Mr Smith 64s 6d per tod, Alfred Lees came with me home and stayed all night, Father trying to open the sough in the little Lydget to let the water off, Thomas thrashing John fetching stone to the Highways.

Saturday 9th.

Went to Chesterfield my Mrs went with me and Mr Mayhew and Alfred Lees allso, Father looking over the cattle and about home, Thomas thrashing John fetching stone to the Highways. Turned the cows into the Meekfield at night, avery fine day.

Sunday 10th.   North East wind and rather cold for the time of year.

Monday 11th.   Went with John and Thomas mowing in the Cowley Lydget, I left about ½ past 9, they finished it I went to Bakewell Market, Father went to the market, got home about 4 oclock went to John and Thomas and mowed a little in the great Lydget, very cold North East wind.

Tuesday 12th.   Went with John and Thomas mowing in the great Lydget finished mowing all that was fit to mow in that field a very poor crop only mowed about half the great Lydget. John

Mowing by hand from L. C. Sequin. Rural England 1885

© Museum of English Rural Life, University of Reading

took the black colt to Mr Barnets pasture at night, took the lambs from the ewes and put them in the croft, Father hay making, North East wind the barometer lowering a little. Some wool came from Halifax by the railway, sent an order for 24 sacks of flour & 22 bran and one ton of fourths.

Wedensday 13th.   Mr Ferguson came I went with him to Mr Platters of Harthill Hall and bought his wool at 70s. per tod all hogg, went to Mr Wains but he had promised his to Hakewell, came Holme and Mr Ferguson left me 192£ 12s. to pay for the wool that I had bought, Father John and Thomas Haymaking at Lydget a very hot day

Thursday 14th.   All of us in the hay at the Lydget finished.gathering in what whe have there, gave Thomas 1£1s.for him to send to

Bringing in the hay
© Mrs Ellis

Ireland, a very hot day.

Friday 15th.	Mowing in the bull balk John helping me, mowed till eleven oclock at night, did nothing in the afternoon Thomas and father haymaking.
Saturday 16th.	Finished mowing the bull balk began at 2 oclock in the morning, Wm. Downs helping us till 5 oclock left John at 7 to finish it. Then I went to Rowsley Station weighing wool and paying for all that I had bought in this neighbourhood Mr Wilson Mr Darbyshire Mr Dakin Mr Robinson and Mr Smith In all 30 tod 13lbs. Amounting in all to [*left a space*]. Then went by the 12 oclock train to Longstone Station got my dinner at Mr Mawnes then went to Mr Lowes but he had sold his wool came home by the 4 oclock train but I felt very poorly, John and Thomas and Father in the hay they got one load when I got home, whe got another load and rowed up the remainder a very excessive hot day.
Sunday 17th.	Went to Holmesfield Feast the Mrs with me and Henry and George. I went to Holmesfield Church in the afternoon, a very hot day.
Monday 18th.	Stoped all night at Mothers weighed and paid for all the wool that I had bought at Holmesfield went to Mr Blands

Haymaking at a Rowsley farm on the Chatsworth Estate
© Julie Bunting

of Barlow and looked at his wool went to Owler Bar to see him but whe could not bargain I offered 70s. per tod. Brother George and me had some words about a sovereign that I lent him last Christmas but one, he denied me ever lending him one but I am quite certain that I did lend him one. Came home at night Father and John and Thomas finished haymaking in the Bull Balk, another very hot day.

Tuesday 19th.
Leading flour and bran and sharps from the station that I had from Thorpe of Newark, Thomas in the turnips another hot day.

Wednesday 20th.
Mowing in the cow close Joseph Evans came at night and helped us a little, Thomas in the turnips a little in the morning then him and Father hay making a very hot day.

Thursday 21st.
Began mowing very early Joseph Evans went with us about one hour mowed till noon a slight shower in the afternoon, Thomas and Father in the hay till noon then they took some thatch to the Lydget in the afternoon. Thomas went in the turnips a little at night, I lent Mr Mayhew 5£, a very dull day barometer falling.

Friday 22nd.
John took some flower [*flour*] to Edensor and Pilsley and went forward for one load of stone for the Highways, got Short shod on one foot at Pilsley as he went. Thomas in the

turnips in the morning then he and I went and got some hay up in the cow close I went to Bakewell Market in the afternoon, Father and John and Tom got some more up in the afternoon, a shower of rain in the afternoon.

Saturday 23rd.
Whe got 2 waggon loads of hay out of the Cow Close, the dukes mowers and Ben Halksworth and John and Wm. Downs came and helped us to finish mowing the Cow Close and teded it, a fine hay day not too hot.

Sunday 24th.
Rather a fine day not too hot.

Monday 25th.
Hay making in the Cow Close lead 3 wagon load it rained a little in the afternoon, John and Thomas mowed the hollow in the Southfield and tedded it.

Tuesday 26th.
John and Thomas in the turnips in the morning then finished getting the hay out of the Cow Close, got 2 more loads Paid Thomas Gannon 3 weeks and 5 days wage at 9s. per week 3£ 14s 6d.

Wedensday 27th.
Rabbiting in cow close caught 7, Father and I and Elizabeth got one load out of the Hollows in South Field Finished our hay. John went to Boythorpe for coal for ourselves a very hot sultry day.

Thursday 28th.
Weighing flour and takeing some out in the morning, John took some flour to Pilsley then went forward for one load of stone for the Highways. Diping the hoggs in the afternoon, Harriatt and S A Bowen and her Mother came to see us, Henry went back with them.

Friday 29th.
Went to the Lydgath in the morning with Father and looked over the gees wanted to have killed one for Mr Mayhew but there was not one good enough, the heaviest $9^3/4$.lbs. Went to Bakewell in the afternoon, John singling turnips.

Saturday 30th.
John leading stone to the Highways with 2 horses, Father thatching at Lydget, I waited till the post came then I walked to Chesterfield, then I went to Barlow to Mr Blands and weighed his wool, 15 tod 8 lbs and paid him for it 55£ then I went to Storth House and stayed there all night a very hot day.

Sunday 31st.
I left Storth House about 10 oclock and rode to Barlow by the coach got home about 1/2 past 12 at noon a slight shower or two of rain but very little.

Monday 1st. August.
John leading stone to the Highways with 2 horses, I and Father and S Ludlam went Rabbitting in the Derwent banks caught 15 rabbits.

Tuesday 2nd.
I went to Mr Wains then I went to Bakewell, came home and started by Rail at 7 oclock for Manchester. John in the

turnips, Father Jobing about home, stayed with Mr A Lees all night.

Wedensday 3rd.

Left Manchester 10 o'clock with Mr A Lees for the Isle of Man arrived at the Isle of Man at 5pm. Met with Mr Anthony and Mr Holmes of King Sterndale. John went to Boythorpe for coal for Rev. G. S. Outram, Father finished thatching at Lydget Brewed 6 pks. of malt.

In margin, Thursday 4th to Sat. 7th John went to Rowsley and get the horse shod, went for stone with two horses in the afternoon for the Highways. John mowing bracken in the far common piece, Lent Mr Outram 1£ still dry weather.

John went to Boythorpe for 2 loads of coal one for Mr Spencer and one for ourselves. Father went to Chesterfield and Mr Johnston looked at Short but did not bargain dry weather.

Sunday 7th.

A day missing.

Monday 8th.

John went for one load of stone for the Highways and took some flour to Edensor in the morning, got the bracken together in the far piece. Father went to Bakewell Market, I returned home on Monday night, left the Isle of Man at 9am., was very sick as I came over and very tired when I got home, I arrived in L.pool about 2pm. Left L.pool at ½ past 4, Rowsley at 10 minutes past 8pm. Brought two cats that Mr Lees had bought one for Mrs Mayhew and the other for the Hill Top.

Tuesday 9th.

Morning, Raining beautifull rain very much wanted, John thrashing most of the day, Wm. began of cutting corn in the South field several showers of rain during the the day. I was very tired after my journey to the Isle of Man, Killed a little pig.

Wednesday 10th.

Richard Stour came at 9s. per week John and Richard thrashing in the morning. I was looking up sacks and mending some went cuting corn in the afternoon a few nice showers of rain in the morning.

Thursday 11th.

Finished cuting the oats at the other side of South Field before noon, fetched our waggon load of bracken out of the far common piece, a hot day.

Friday 12th.

Went to Darley settled with Mr Else to the 24th June paid him for 1 tod 7lbs. of wool 3£ 18s. Mr Mayhew paid me the 5£ and I borrowed 4£ of him, paid John Smith 1s. tor newspaper commencing on 30th July I went to Bakewell in the afternoon set 4 score of Salery [*celery?*] plants at night, John and Richard thrashing and jobing about home, a very hot day.

Saturday 13th.	I and Father and John and Richard cuting oats in the wood close an uncommon hot day, I was very poorly in the afternoon.
Sunday 14th.	Went to Baslow feast and brought Henry home with me, Mr Ludlam went with me, another very hot day.
Monday 15th.	Mr Ludlam and two of his men helping us cut oats in the wood close, a very fine day rather cooler. I sent an order for 24 sacks of flour & 10 cwt. of sharps and 3 ton of bran the bran at 5s.4d. per cwt.
Tuesday 16th.	Mr Ludlam and 2 of his men helping us cut oats in the Bering gate, rather a sultry day not much sun.
Wedensday 17th.	Got one stack of oats in the morning John Ludlam picking on the stack, Mr Ludlam and 2 of his men helping us to finish cuting oats in the south field, caught 7 rabbits and one old hare, finished cuting except about 5 roods of wheat, a very good crop of oats in the South Field and middling crop in wood close, the game had made very hard work in the hiring gate, eaten it all in some places.
Thursday 18th.	John and Richard raking fetched the rakings home out of the far side of the South Field in the morning. Father covering the stack that was made yesterday, Jim Buckley reached him the thatch, leading the rakings out of the wood close at night, rather a gloomy day very little air.
Friday 19th.	I fetched 4 loads of flour and offals from Rowsley Station in the morning, John and Richard helping Mr Ludlam to cut oats all day, I and Father helping him in the afternoon.
Saturday 20th.	John and Richard helping Mr Ludlam all day. I was jobing about in the morning helping to draw a steam engine to Bunkers Hill with 2 horses in the afternoon for Mr Drabble, charged 5s.for helping them, a very close day.
Sunday 21st.	Morning thunder and lightning and some very nice rain, rained at intervals all day, more rain this day than whe have had for some months past I think since April.
Monday 22nd.	Went to Bakewell Market, John and Richard helping Mr Ludlam cut oats, Father jobing about home I ordered 6 bags of flour of Mr Else to have 1d. per stone returned of the 1s 10d. per stone. 30 pks. at 32s 6d. 2 bags bean meal 19s 6d. per bag 16 stone, a dry day
Tuesday 23rd.	John and Richard helping Mr Ludlam they caught 10 rabbits when cuting corn, I looked 20 sacks and sent to Newark for bran, Wm. Mountney fetched 2 pigs paid me for them 8£ 5s. I sent 30£ to Newark for Messrs. Thorpe & Co., a few light showers.
Wedensday 24th.	Began shearing the wheat all of us Joseph Reding and

	Joseph Evans helped at night, the valuers came over the wheat while we were shearing, a fine harvest day.
Thursday 25th.	Leading oats all day, got 10 waggon loads put 6 waggon loads in the wood brandery out of the wood close and the hiring gate, 2 waggon loads in the barn and left 2 loads on the waggons, the middle brandery came of the far side of the South Field poland oats, and one load out of the wood close Freeslands, a fine harvest day.
Friday 26th.	John and Richard finished rakeing and lead the rakeings, finished getting all our oats, Father and I went to Bakewell Fair a fine harvest day.
Saturday 27th.	Wm. Downs John and Richard went shearing in the morning I went to little brook and took the stirks to the Lydget brought the gees from the Lydget and the Hoggs out of the Morton Greave and took them in the wood close and hiring gate, then helped the others to finish shearing caught 3 rabbits and one leverit, Father covering the stack that was made on Thursday, a fine harvest day. Paid R Stour 1£ 4s.for 2 weeks wage.
Sunday 28th.	Went to Thornbridge with my Mrs. Stayed there till night then went to Ashford and stayed there all night, a few showers of rain.
Monday 29th.	I and the Mrs stayed at Ashford all day, bought Mr P Furniss wool 65s 6d. per tod. John went to Pilsley with the cart to have the wheels hached and one fore waggon wheel to have to feller put in. Helping Mr Ludlam in the afternoon, a few showers of rain.
Tuesday 30th.	John and Father and I finished thrashing the old oats and thrashed all the rakings, then fixed the chopper and chopped some straw for the cows and some for the horses, began to give the cows two fodderings of chop and bran and a little bean meal in it, John went to Pilsley for the cart at night, a very fine day but barometer falling.
Wedensday 31st.	John went to Boythorpe with 2 carts for coal 1 ton for Mr Outram and 15 cwt. for ourselves. Jobing about in the morning went to the smithy and got the young horse shod in the afternoon.
Thursday 1st. Sept.	Fetched 4 loads of flour and bran from Rowsley Station, then chopped some for the horses and cows. John went to the Feast in the afternoon I went and helped Mr Ludlam to finish cuting oats.
Friday 2nd.	John went to Boythorpe for coal 1 ton for Mr Outram, 16cwt. for ourselves. I and Father not doing much, a few showers of rain fell during the day.
Saturday 3rd.	Winnowing 5 qrs. of the old oats. D Milmes came from

AGRICULTURAL PROSPECTS IN DERBYSHIRE.—
On Sunday morning week, about seven o'clock,
North Derbyshire was visited by a severe thun-
derstorm. The peals of thunder were very loud,
and the flashes of lightning very vivid. The
rain, which was much wanted, descended in tor-
rents. The rain has done good. The remaining
part of the week has been hot and dry, and very
favourable for harvest operations, and corn cutting is going on in all directions in Derbyshire
in good earnest. Seldom or ever was a finer sea-
son experienced in this locality for the ingather-
ing of the crops; and in the south part of Derbyshire a good portion of the corn is already safely
housed. In the north a fair quantity of corn has
been stacked, but the greater bulk is still stand-
ing. The root crops are drooping for want of a
further supply of rain, and it is feared that they
will, in nine cases out of ten, prove a failure. The
nights during he past week have been very frosty.
This will materially help to ripen the outstand-
ing corn in the Peak of Derbyshire; and if fine
weather continues, no doubt the whole of the corn
will be safely stacked, and housed in about ten
days. As regards the wheat crop the accounts
vary: in some places it is pretty good, while in
others there will be a deficiency. The barley
crop turns out better than expected. Beans vary
in some parts the yield will be good, in other
parts very poor. Oats in most parts of Derbyshire are this year proving a poor crop, the grain
being poorly fed and the straw very short. Farmers in North Derbyshire are still busily engaged carting water from the rivers to keep their
cattle alive.

The weather and the crops in 1864
Derbyshire Times 3 September 1864

Ashford and tried to buy 8 lambs, he bid 24s 6d. each, I offered them at 25s each. Father getting a few early potatose, rain at night

Sunday 4th.   A fine day.

Monday 5th.   Went to Rowsley Station with Mr Mayhew then chopped a good deal for the horses and cows, then lead wheat out of the south field and made it in a stack and put 2 waggon loads of oats on it finished all our corn, I went to Baslow with gearing [*harness*] to be mended, took my boots to Mr Bodens to be mended and paid him last years bill, Paid Mr Hodgkinson for 20 pks. of malt, A Lees went with me a very rough wind all day.

Tuesday 6th.   John went to Boythorpe for coal for Mr Spencer of Edensor 1ton 16cwt. Father and Kent rabbiting in cow close caught 12.

Wedensday 7th.   John cleaning up the yard I went to Rowsley with Bute and Boxer to be shod, Father began thatching.

Thursday 8th.   John went to Boythorpe for coal, one ton for Mr Outram and 16cwt. for ourselves, I was jobing about finished getting the early potatose.

Friday 9th.   John went to Boythorpe for coal one ton for Mr Outram and 16cwt. for ourselves, I was helping Mr Ludlam lead oats, went with my Uncle Charles to Rowsley Station in the morning.

Saturday 10th.   I put the young horse in the chains with Joseph Evans went 3 times to Rowsley then put him in the light cart and went to Darley Mill for one bag Ind. Meal and one bag bean meal, Paid Mrs Else 5£ John leading manure in the south field.

Sunday 11th.   I went up to see Mr Lees this afternoon. Mrs George Lees died this morning.

Monday 12th.   Went to Edensor in the morning then went to Bakewell in the afternoon with the young horse, walked forward to Ashford, John leading manure in the south field, Father went to Bakewell Mr Mayhew came from London.

Tuesday 13th.   John went to Boythorpe for coal for ourselves 1 ton 17cwt. I went to Chatsworth with Mr Mayhew and a few more to meet Mr Cottingham to consult about the coal on Beeley Moor what steps should be taken, whe agree to test the mines by Boring, the Duke agrees to pay half the expens if no coal can be found.

Wedensday 14th.   I had the breaking tackle on Mr Mayhews horse. John finished leading manure in the south field, a very rainy afternoon John riddle chaff in the afternoon

Thursday 15th.	Had the breaking tackle on Mr Mayhews horse went to Rowsley with it, then thrashing and choping a little at night, a good deal of rain during last night.
Friday 16th.	Choping in the morning then went to the cattle show at Derby went into the corn market bought 15qrs. of Indian corn of Mr Heighton of Nottingham at 30s. per qr at Gloster. Wm. Downs went with me, John spreading manure.
Saturday 17th.	Winnowing 5qrs.of oats then took them to the mill bought 5 bags of Indian meal of Mr Martins at 19s. per sack and 3 sacks of bean meal at 1£ per bag, took Mr Halksworth Lees 1 bag of flour & 5 stone of Ind. Meal, Helped Mrs Mayhew saddle her young horse she went with us to the mill and to the Lees. John spreading manure the day out.Father thatching.
Sunday 18th.	A fine day.
Monday 19th.	Father and Henry took 8 sheep and 8 lambs to Bakewell Market, I went by Pilsley and took Mr Holmes 10 stone Ind. Meal then went to Bakewell and stood with the sheep but could not sell them dummy [damme?], brought them home. John spreading manure.
Tuesday 20th.	Choping in the morning then went to Bakewell for a witness for Thomas Froggatt, in a horse case which he had sold to a farmworker of Matlock Mr Froggatt won the case. Father thatching John spreading manure.
Wedensday 21st.	Looking sacks up and mending and marking some with my name, sent of 26 of Thorpes and 30 of mine off to Newark. Sent Messrs. Thorpe 30£ and an order for 1 ton bran and 1 ton sharps and 26 sacks of flour, John spreading manure in the mains Father thatching.
Thursday 22nd.	Went to the Hill Top John with me diping sheep, diped of ours 53 sheep.
Friday 23rd.	Choping until noon then went and got a few potatose John with me, Father thatching finished and finished haring? the stacks.
Saturday 24th.	Straightening about home in the morning putting the harvest waggon by and all the shelvings and the rollers then all of us went and got potatose the remainder of the day. Went to Rowsley at night to meet Mr Mayhew he came from London by the 10 o'clock train.
Sunday 25th.	A beautifull fine day.
Monday 26th.	Fetched 4 loads of flour from Rowsley Station, Father and Mrs and John went to Chesterfield Fair.
Tuesday 27th.	I went to Sheffield went with Mother to the Bank she got

the interest of 80£ which is in the Sheffield and Rotherham Bank righted she drew the shillings and left the 3£ to the 80£ making a totall of 83£. Father and John jobing about.

Wedensday 28th. Choping in the morning, fetching Indian Corn and bran and sharps from Rowsley Station. I went to Bakewell to Mr Greaves with 5 gees at 5s. each at night. Sold Mr Parker the chees at 67s per cwt.

Thursday 29th. John went to Edensor mill then went to Edensor for 2 loads of manure for Wm. Downs, then went to Rowsley Station for the remaining Indian Corn. John getting potatose in the afternoon beautifull fine weather, very hot.

Friday 30th. John potato getting I jobing about home in the morning, went to Bakewell in the afternoon the Mrs went with me.

Saturday 1st. Oct. Choping and thrashing and cleaning up, finished thrashing all the corn that was in the barn.

Sunday 2nd. Had a goose to our dinner.

Monday 3rd. I went to Bakewell Market then went forward to Ashford and came home by the 8 o'clock train, John ploughing the Bering gate for fallow next year, Father got a few potatose.

Tuesday 4th. Went to Rowsley in the morning to get some irons altered and some hooks and staples made, John ploughing in the morning and we did some choping in the afternoon and

In Church Lane, Rowsley. 'Went to Rowsley in the morning'
© J. Jones

shot some Indian corn and sent the railway sacks off.

Wedensday 5th. John ploughing I was making bills out in the morning, went to Edensor and Pilsley with flour &e and recvd. Mr Halls and Mr Spencers and Mrs Turners and Mr Buckleys bills, then went to Bakewell with a cow to be ready for the show tied her in Mr Ormes cowhouse at night.

Thursday 6th. Father and I went to the cattle show with some hens and one cock 2 gees[e] and one gander and 6lbs butter, took the second prize for the butter but got no other prize. The cow

BAKEWELL FARMERS' CLUB.

The annual exhibition of farming stock and produce, promoted by the members of the Bakewell Farmers' Club, was held on the 6th, inst. The weather was all that could be desired, and there was a considerable number of visitors from the surrounding villages, and from Chesterfield, Matlock, and Buxton. The club has now reached its sixteenth year, and it is admitted by all practical farmers that it has been the means of effecting great good by exciting a healthy spirit of competition in their midst. This show was in some respects not is well supported as some of its predecessors, there being a falling off in point of numbers in several classes; but it was also true that the quality of the animals and the produce exhibited had not at all deteriorated. Some very useful animals were shown in the classes for horses; and it seems that increasing attention is being given to the breeding of a good sound class of hunters, for what we may term "home consumption" in this thoroughly hunting district. The poultry classes exhibited a large increase over last year; and the prizes offered for competition by cottagers were keenly contested. Altogether, the show was considered to be a very satisfactory one. It was visited by Lord Geo. Cavendish, M.P., Lord Denman, Sir Joseph Paxton, M.P., and many other gentlemen of influence in the district. The judges were :—For cattle and sheep—Mr. Lowe, Tapton; Mr. Maskery, Norbury. For horses and pigs—Mr. R. Crofts, Staveley; Mr. J. Milnes, West Hallam. For poultry— Mr. T. P. Wood, Jun. For cheese and butter--Mr. Cox, Derby. General referee—Mr. John Noton, Edensor.

The annual dinner was served, as usual, at the Rutland Arms, and Mr. Greaves provided for the comfort of his guests, in his well-known style. About 120 sat down to dinner.

Account of Bakewell Show in the Bakewell Standard 14th October 1864

a very good Roan cow was unsuckfull!, I dined with members of the Club, John about home untill 11 o'clock then went to Bakewell for the cow, Father and Mrs brought the fowls home. I paid Mr Furniss 5£ on account of some wool that I bought of him about one month since.

Friday 7th.

Went with John and ploughed the remainder of the potatose out, then weighed and loaded the chees to go to Chesterfield tomorrow, John finished gathering the potatose, I went to Ashford in the afternoon with 4 bags of Ind. Meal and 1 sack of Indian corn and received the money for it, very dry weather.

Saturday. 8th.

Went to Chesterfield John took the chees and brought 1 ton of coal and 7cwt. of slack from Boythorpe. I went with Mr Ludlam and came back with him, the chees weighed just the same as it did at home 12cwt. 2qrs. and 19lbs. recvd. 42£ 7s 9d. for the chees lent Mr Mason 1£ Paid him all that I owed him.

Monday 10th.

Choping a little broke the choper, Father took it to Ashover to Mr Cundy to be repaired, I and Henry went on Calton for the young cattle left them in Chatsworth Park to stop till the end of this month. I went to Edensor and paid 4£ 15s. for the adgistment of the cattle on calton, got half of a stack in in the afternoon John carried water for the calves and fodered the sheep. Mr Lees came at night and paid his acct.

Tuesday 11th.

Sent a Telegraph message for Mr Mayhew paid 2s 6d. for it, thrashing about an hour then sent John to Eyam to Joshua Blackwell with 10 hoggs for the winter. Took Mr Deeley 10st. flour & 1 sack Ind. Meal then went to Birchover to Mr Heathcoat and bought one shearling ram of him gave 3£ 12s 6d. and 2s return, Mr Lees went with me. Sent a check to Newark for Messrs Thorpe & Co for 59£ 2s. Father fetched the black colt from the woodhouse.

Wedensday 12th.

Winnowing some oats sent them to the mill 3qrs and 2 qrs. of Ind corn, John took the stirks in the Park. Father went to Ashover for the chopper got two loads of coal in and made ready for to do some chopping. Chopped a little and then the Mrs and I went to Manchester, Mr A Lees met us at the station, the Wesleyans had a tea in the schoolroom about 200 of us sat down to tea.

Thursday 13th.

I was Mr A Lees all day. my Mrs went and stayed with Miss Emma Milnes her cousin, until Friday night, then whe got ready on the Saturday morning to go to Liverpool.

Friday 14th.

With Mr Lees most of the day, went to Mr Woodruff Pork Butcher in Danes Gate and bought 8 pots of lard of him

paid him 6¼d per lb for it half of it for Mr D Milnes of Ashford.

Saturday 15th.   Whe arrived in Liverpool about half past 9 in the morning, went to the Old Swan to Mr Travis dined with them, then the Mr and Mrs went with us to Liverpool and whe took the boat for New Brighton, came back to Liverpool and called to see Fred Potts then went and stayed with Mr Travis at their home.

Sunday 16th. Mr Travis and I went to church in the morning, Edwin Vickers called in the afternoon and whe had a walk.

Monday 17th. I went to the cattle market in the morning and saw a very great market I should think many thousands of sheep and cattle, then went back to Mr Travis and had breakfast, then whe all went to Liverpool and Mr Travis and I went into Great Omer St. to Mr G Walls, I bought a firkin of butter of him. My Mrs and Mrs Travis whe left in the museum until whe came back, whe all looked about Liverpool and in the Docks then went and got tea with Mr Travis and went to the Limestreet Station and left Liverpool for Manchester arrived in Manchester about 8pm. My Mrs went to her cousin and I stoped with Mr Travis all night.

Tuesday 18th. We left Manchester by the 2pm. Train got to Ashford at 4, bought one pig of S. Manning at 5s 6d per stone got home at 8pm.

Wedensday 19th. John finished ploughing in the hiring gate then whe took Mr Mayhews pony and put between two of our and harrowed with them till night.

Thursday 20th. John spreading manure in the southfield I had Mr Mayhews horse in the light cart, whe choped a little in the morning Father jobing about home, it rained very heavy in the night.

Friday 21st. John harrowing in the Bering gate I took two hoggs into Henry Halksworths field for the winter and one into G Bonds field. Bought Mr Outhams hay stack for 14£ and one bracken stack for 10s. went to Bakewell in the afternoon with Mr Mayhew had his pony in the cart.

Saturday 22nd. Went and put the calves in Wm. Browns field at 1s.each per week 6 of them, finished thrashing all there is in the

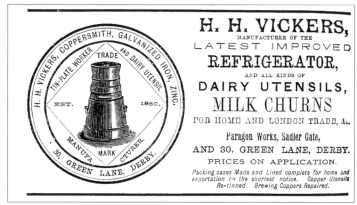

Rutland Square, Bakewell. 'Went to Bakewell in the afternoon with Mr Mayhew'
© Derbyshire Libraries

barn then choping a little. Paid Marsden the land and assess? taxes, a good deal of rain during the night and the first part of the day.

Sunday 23rd.
Got a very bad cold.

Monday 24th.
John nocking manure I and Father went to Matlock fair Paid Mr Barnet 2£ 12s. for 13 weeks keep of the Black horse at 4d. per week.

Tuesday 25th.
Fetching flour from Rowsley Station and 1 ton of fourths and ½. ton of bran let Mr Mortimer have 1 ton, went to Pilsley in the afternoon with Mr Mayhew home in the light cart and our young one to be school, took Mr Holmes and Mr Hawley some flour & pig stuff.

Wedensday 26th.
John finished nocking manure in the south field in the morning fetched the calves down for Mr Shenton to Seaton? John and Father fetched the Bracking stack out of Mr Outhams croft. I fetched 12 ewes and turned them to the ram one tuped at night, sent half notes and check to Messrs. Sturge of Birmingham for 22£10s. when completed.

Thursday 27th.
Been a very wet night John took the calves back into Browns field, then choping sticks then cleaning up. Not doing much myself had the tackle on Mr Mayhew's young horse, then choping in the afternoon.

Friday 28th.
John leading manure into the great lydget, then riddling hayseeds in the afternoon, I went to Bakewell.

Saturday 29th.
John leading manure into the south field, George Downs came down and bought 4 shares at 35s. each and sent for

Horse fair at Matlock Green. 'I and Father went to Matlock Fair'
© Mrs Ellis

them at night. I went up to Edensor at night, Mrs Milnes paid me their bill, I went to Jepsons to have settled with them but he had not made the bill out, Mr Lees was with them whe came home together gave 10s. Mr Outhams testimonial.

Sunday 30th.   A very fine day for the time of the year, Aunt and Ellen Milnes came from Ashford and stayed all night.

Monday 31st.   I went to Edensor and settled with Mr Jepson up to this time he sent me one sack 4 bushels of malt at 60s. per qr. Got home about noon Father and John choping. John took 3 qrs. of Indian corn to Edensor Mill then he went spreading manure in the south field in the afternoon.

NOVEMBER 1864 – APRIL 1865

In this six months we read of the autumn and winter work on the farm, and of the disagreement with the Chatsworth agent Mr Cottingham. Although this is resolved, we are left with the feeling of wanting to know more about the situation.

The departure of the Vicar, Mr Outram seems to have been an emotional affair, and it isn't long before there is disagreement with the new incumbent the Revd. Sculthorpe. The reference to this on the 1st January 1865 was written in the margin across other writing, which has made deciphering it extremely hard. Only just in time, before going to print, and with the aid of the computer was the meaning revealed.

William refers to sending half notes to suppliers of goods. Presumably this was done for security reasons. I wonder when this practise ceased, it can't have been very popular with banks, having to deal with quantities of notes cut in half and the problem of matching up numbers.

The reference to carting slags, probably refers to taking slags from the old lead smelting sites for resmelting in more efficient works elsewhere.

I was thrilled to find the entry referring to President Lincoln. My Mother had told me that it was included in the diary. The transatlantic cable was in operation by this date, but the news still took a while to circulate around the country.

Tuesday 1st. Nov.	Getting half of a oat stack in, I belted 13 more sheep and turned them to the ram 11 of them tupt. S Mawrey brought a fat pig that I had bought of him, made a thatch stack, John went to Edensor Mill and fetched the Indian meal, the cow club meeting at night paid 16s. subscription.
Wedensday 2nd.	John went to finish nocking manure in the south field, I went to Rowsley then came back the blacksmiths beasts was in our turnips, then came home and killed the pig that S Mawrey brought yesterday. Began making a pigeon coat in the hay barn, went to Mr Outhams at night and he settled with me, I paid him 1£ 10s.for rent for bracking stack and 1£ 4s. for newspapers up to Christmas and 5£ on acct. for the hay stack remaining due to Mr Outham 9£.
Thursday 3rd.	John went and began pulling turnips took the beast one load of tops and brought one load of bottom home. I was making the pigeon coat a little, cut up and weighed the pig it weighed 24st. 13lbs. George Downs came and paid for the sheep that he bought 7£ I gave him 1s. for luck. Choping a little.
Friday 4th.	Working at the pigeon coat part of the day, jobing about some part of the day, sent the barn door lock by John Smith to Sheffield to have a new key. John went pulling turnips in the morning then went and finished nocking manure in the great lydget.
Saturday 5th.	John leading two loads of turnips tops, one load for today and one load for Sunday that is tomorrow, he went and pulled some more in the afternoon, whe choped some for the cows I was working at the pigeon coat part of the day nearly finished the wood work ordered a window frame of Mr Holmes of Pilsley. John Smith brought the lock back from Sheffield and a new key.
Sunday 6th.	Mr Outram administered the Holy Communion twice this day and he preached a very affecting sermon to a very full church and made many of his hearers weep and bid his hearers farewell.
Monday 7th.	John took the cows one load of turnip tops then him and I winnowed 5 qrs. of oats then he took 4 qrs. to the mill and

one sack of light ones to be split for the horses, I took some orders out, took Mr Mayhew 1 sack of oats. John went pulling turnips I went and helped Mr Outram to load some goods Sarah Buckley called with Mr Outrams children and bid me farewell. Father went to Bakewell to the ???? to an extraordinary meeting of the Board of Guardians.

Tuesday 8th.

Sold turner and the young Bull to [*left a space*], for the sum of 13£ to go on Friday, next he had bid me 23£ for the best cow that whe took to the cattle show. Helping Mr Outram to the station with the light cart full of lugage, thay went by the 11 am. Train, helped to load 2 loads of furniture in the afternoon belonging to Mr Outram. I took John Elliott 1/2. Bag of flour and 2 qrt of parafin oil went to Edensor at night to the Chatsworth Farmers Club. John puling turnips most of the day whe choped some for the horses in the morning, Father jobing about most of the day.

Wedensday 9th.

Mountney fetched the 2 pigs that I sold him last Friday he paid for them 7£ 19s. I went to Ashford to appeal against

Boy walking up Hill Cross, Ashford-in-the-Water. Late 19th century.
© Derbyshire County Council

the Income Tax, I got off. Settled with D Mines up to this time, Father and John puling turnips part of the day John took Mr Lees 10 st. of flour. Recd. a letter from Mr Heighton of Nottingham with samples and prices of corn.

Thursday 10th.

Recvd. Several lots of money and righted John Halksworth and Windles books, took some flour to Halksworth paid me 1£ 10s, called at the mill for the meal from the oats that went to the mill on Monday, fetched 2 loads of turnips out of the Bering gate, had 19st. of bean meal of Mr Mortimer, John puling turnips Father helping him a little.

Friday 11th.

John went to Boythorpe for 2 tons of coal for Mr Spencer, I was jobing about in the morning went to Bakewell in the afternoon with Mr Mayhew took him home in the light cart, lent Mr Mayhew 10s. Father jobing about home.

Saturday 12th.

Went to Pilsley with flour and met Mr Youngs traveler with short but he did not think him good enoughf, got home about noon. John Downs making a hole in the top of the hay barn for a window and put it in the pigeon coat Father helping him, part of the day. John and I helping him part of the afternoon, John and I fetched the young cattle out of Park, Father fetched the calves out of Wm. Browns field and put them into the Mortin Greave. I and Father went to Mr Mayhews at night, Mr Sculthorpe the clergyman came to Beeley I had an interview with him.

Sunday 13th.

Rather a wet day, Mr Sculthorpe preached for the first time in Beeley Church.

Monday 14th.

I and Father went to Bakewell Fair Market, Holmes went with us whe took the young horse in the light cart. John fetched Mr Sculthorpe 1 ton of hard coal from Bodens of Rowsley, then he took Short to the Fair but did not sell him.

Tuesday 15th.

I finished making the pigeon coat except hinging the door. John Downs came and finished pitching the race round the thrashing machine Father helping him a little, John pulling turnips I went to Bakewell in the afternoon to fetch some hardware and pots and glasses for Mr Sculthorpe. Got home about 6 o'clock.

Wedensday 16th.

Fetched the sheep home and marked them took them into the Morton Greave, choping in the morning, John cleaning the yard untill noon he went pulling turnips in the afternoon. John Cooker took 4 fat choop to kill, sold thom at 8s. per lb. I and Father went pulling turnips in the afternooon, whe finished pulling and fetched 3 loads of bottoms home. Mrs went to the Hill Top, I went to fetch her home at night.

Thursday 17th.	A Very wet day John took the cows a load of turnip tops and brought one load of bottoms home, not doing much but jobing about remainder part of the day
Friday 18th.	Thrashing in the morning, I went to Edensor in the afternoon and paid the rent, went to Mr Cockers and saw the 4 sheep weighed they came to 9£ 5s. 4d. the four. Recvd. 26£ 16s. for game damage, John riddling the oats that whe thrashed this morning, Father looking the cattle and sheep.
Saturday 19th.	I and W. Lees and Isaac Grindy and Father went rabbiting caught 6 in the morning, W Lees and I went in the afternoon and caught 2, I found a fezant in the edge of Cow Close, John Cocker paid for the 4 sheep 9£ 5s.
Sunday 20th.	A fine November day rain towards night, A Lees called at night sound[ed] rather on the spree.
Monday 21st.	John leading manure with 2 horses, I led one load of turnip tops for the cows then took Boxer to Rowsley and got him shod John had Short hanged down in the shafts with a load of manure. Luke Hadfield came and I sold him the Great Cow for the sum of 24£ to go tomorrow or next day. Mrs Bown came and paid what they owed to this date, S Downs paid up to this date allso I wrote to Newark for the price of flour & sent Mr Travis a newspaper, did some choping in the afternoon.
Tuesday 22nd.	John leading manure on the butts in the morning, spreading a little in the afternoon. Old Mr Holmes took very ill had a kind of stroke, Father there most of the afternoon. I went to the sale at Meadow Place to the late Mrs Gregorys place, things sold very dear, a wet uncomfortable day.
Wedensday 23rd.	John spread the manure that he lead out and nocked a little, he left us I paid him the balance due to him. I sent half notes to Messrs. Thorpe of Newark for 50£ sent an order for flour and offals 20 sacks SSS, 4 sacks A 3 tons of bran 1 ton fourths, Luke Hadfield sent for the cow that I sold him, Old Mr Holmes still very ill wrote a letter to Mr Travis.
Thursday 24th.	Looking up sacks and mending and sent 26 of Thorpes and 50 of mine to Newark, Father at old Mr Holmes most of the day Old Mr Holmes died in the afternoon, borrowed 1/4 lb of twine of Mr Mortimer for mending sacks.
Friday 25th.	I went to Chesterfield fair to[ok] Short and showed him but did not sell him. Paid Mr Mason 3£ for Mr Mayhew, Mr Mason paid me 1£ that I lent him some since. Mr Mayhew paid with 3£ that I paid to Mr Mason for him. I got home

about half past 5 o'clock A very stormy rough night.

Saturday 26th.
1 went ploughing a little in the morning Father went with me I had the young mare in the plough the first time she went very nicely, I received an invoice from Newark of the flour that I sent for and of 15cwt. of bran and 10cwt. of fourths. Paid Mr Cundy 16s 6d. for mending the chopper, a stormy day.

Sunday 27th.
A very fine day, Old Mr Holmes was intered this day aged 82 years.

Monday 28th.
I went to Bakewell Market a very wet day, paid one years insurance money up to Oct. 1st. 1865, Paid Mr Else of Darley Mill 15£ on acct. for fourths I had. Fetched 2 loads of flour and offal from Rowsley station at night.

Tuesday 29th.
Fetched the remaining 2 loads from Rowsley Station of fourths &e. Delivered several lots out went to Pilsley in the afternoon with some flour ½. Bag to Mr Holmes and 1 bag to S Noton. Recd. of Mrs Noton 1£ on acct.. Choping a little in the afternoon, Aaron Stevenson came at 6s. per week he was nocking manure, My Mrs went to the Hill Top, I went to fetch her from Mr W Lees at night.

Wedensday. 30th.
Went ploughing a little in the morning very wet afternoon

'Fetched the remaining 2 loads from Rowsley Station'

not doing much, Aaron jobing about most of the day mended 5 sacks.

Thursday 1st. Dec. Went and carried some sticks out of the plantation, Aaron did, I took the cart down and brought a good load home brought a ash pole to make a swingletree of I was making one and cut my foot with the aze, I am very lame tonight I lost a good deal of blood, Father and Aaron winnowing in the afternoon, a very fine day for the time of year.

Friday 2nd. Father and Aaron getting a stack in I helped them a little, Father fetched a sheep home out of the wood close, it could not stand I killed it and skinned it sold J Cocker the skin for 6s 6d. my foot is a good deal better.

Saturday 3rd. Thrashed the oats that they got in yesterday Isaac Grindey helping us, Aaron tied some straw up in the afternoon. Received an invoice from Newark of 10cwt. fourths and 45cwt. bran, a fine day.

Sunday 4th. I went to Bakewell at night for some medicine for the young horse, Croup? Got a ball for her and gave it her.

Monday 5th. Went to Rowsley with 2 swingletrees to be ironed but they could not do it, called at John Elliott and he settled with me up to this date, Father and Aaron finished tying straw up and cleaned up the oats. Sent a check for 3£ 10s. to the parafin Light Company at Birmingham, lent A Lees 2s. & I went with him to Rowsley Station at night he took a cask with him to Mr Woodruff Pork Butcher, Manchester, to be filled with lard for me, a beautiful fine day. I fetched the calves out of Morton Greave as I was going for them the Duke of Devonshire past me he was going to the shooters in Beeley.

Tuesday 6th. Went to Rowsley Station for the bran and fourths let Mr Mortimer have one ton, called at the smithy for the swingletrees fetched the plough out of the Wood Close, Aaron thrashing a little wheat in the morning, he and Father went with me in the far common piece end helped me begin ploughing in the afternoon, borrowed a collar for Short his is too little, wrote a letter to Mr Jackson of Hull for the price of cake.

Wedensday 7th. Went ploughing in the common piece in the morning, looked 13 gallons of parafin oil for D Milnes of Ashford. Thrashing wheat in the afternoon with the machine, recd. a letter from the Parafin light company Receipt for 3£ 10s., Shenton called and looked at the young mare he gave her a ball, ordered us to rub her head with oils, it is very much swolen on one side. Very wet night but it has been a very fine day, John Cocker took 2 sheep to kill those I sold him some time since to be weighed tomorrow night.

Thursday 8th.	Went to Rowsley for one ton of coals for the Rev. Sculthorpe, Father went to Bakewell to receive poundage for collecting Income Tax for last year. Aaron shaked the straw and cleaned the wheat up Choping in the afternoon, a very deal of rain fell during last night and this morning, went to Edensor to Mr Cocker and saw the sheep weighed.
Friday 9th.	Went ploughing in the far common piece in the morning Father and Aaron winnowing, Aaron took 6qrs. of oats for good meal and one sack to be ground for the horses to Baslow mill in the afternoon, I and Father choping and pulping turnips and mixing chop. Mrs went to Bakewell with Mr Lees, received my Policy for insurance in the United Kingdom Insurance Office for 200£ payable at my death. Sent an order to Mr Jackson of Hull for 2 tons of linseed cake.
Saturday 10th.	Ploughing all day in the far piece Aaron with me all day, Father with us in the morning, a young man called at night wanting a place as servant I engaged him to come one month on trial at 11£ per till Martinmas next 1865, his name is Wm. Holmes from Ambergate. Mr A Lees was at Beeley very drunk I went to the Hill Top with him at night, John Cocker paid for the sheep 4£ gave 1s. for luck.
Sunday 11th.	A fine day, did not go to church.
Monday 12th.	W. and I in the far common piece ploughing till noon, Father went to Bakewell Market, William jobing about in the afternoon. Killed G. Holmes a pig went to Rowsley with the plough irons, saw G Wilson at night he was drunk and a great fool.
Tuesday 13th.	I was ploughing all day in the far common piece, William with me till noon he went to Baslow mill in the afternoon, Henry went with him, Father with me all day. Recvd. A letter from J.G. Cottingham saying that if whe ploughed the far common piece up he should not allow any game damages.
Wedensday 14th.	Wrote a letter to J.G. Cottingham, Sir, having recd. a letter from you yesterday respecting a grass field as you call it that I am ploughing up adjoining Beeley Plantation. Will you kindly inform me on what grounds you object a lowering and Game Damages for the same. This field is doing me no good as it is, another year or two it would be no better than the wild common, it is now growing over with heath and gorse. If I must not plough it, what must I do with it, I think it hath cost me money enoughf allready without having the expens of tilling it again in a few more

years: that field alone hath cost me more than 100£ tilling and fencing. I have done enoughf in that field for it to be my own, Therefore if there is no Game damages I shall not expect to receive any but if there is any damages done I certainly shall expect you to pay for all the damage there is done.

Mr Norman had one dozen pigeons, William ploughing in the far piece Father with him most of the day, I fetched one ton of linseed cake from Rowsley Station, Aaron helped me unload it, he was thrashing most of the day, my back is very lame. Mr H Lees and Mr Thompson had each ½ ton of cake, Mr Thompson paid me for his.

Thursday 15th. Aaron thrashing William ploughing Father went with him I went with them in the morning and helped them to finish a furrow and set another ridge, I was jobing about the rest of the day.

Friday 16th. Father went with William ploughing. Recvd. A letter from Mr Cottingham in answer to the one I wrote yesterday, he asked us to give up our farm at Lady day next or at Lady day 1866 if whe prefered it. I called on him in the afternoon at Chatsworth and he arranged to see the field early part of next week. I went to Bakewell after I had been to Chatsworth, Mr Swain paid me 6£ for damages done by the rabits in the Cow Close, a very cold day.

Cattle in the park at Chatsworth
© Derbyshire County Council

Saturday 17th.	Aaron and William finished thrashing wheat then whe winnowed 9 loads of wheat then did some choping, whe tied the stirks up, I am very lame of my back, I fell down twice the pain was so severe, some snow fell during last night and most of the day snow continued to fall, sent a check 12£10s. to Mr Jackson of Hull for 2 tons of Linseed cake and half of 5£ note 17£10s.
Sunday 18th.	My back is a little better, winterly day a good deal of snow fallen.
Monday 19th.	Getting part of the last stack in, William and Father and I. Aaron came and I paid him for the time he worked for us 11s.4d. for two weeks and 5 days, a friend of Mrs Mayhew's stayed all night at our home he and Mr A Lees went to the 7pm train to night, they had been at Mayhews all day.
Tuesday 20th.	William cleaned up the yard in the morning, I took some flower [sic] out then looked up 17 of Thorpes sacks and 20 of mine and took them to Rowsley Station, sent Mr Jackson the remaining half notes to complete 17£ 10s. for cake. Wrote a letter to Mr A Lees at Manchester asking him to see after the lard for me, I went to the Hill Top at night and Mr H Lees settled with me up to this date. Whe was thrashing this afternoon with the machine.
Wedensday 21st.	Marsden called and wanted us to lead some slags out of the Park to Rowsley Station, William and I took 2 carts and went twice to Rowsley 3 tons 16cwt, 2qrs. at 1s 9d per ton. William tying straw up the remainder of the day, Father helping him. I wrote an order for a cask of Parafin oil, and sent half notes to Messrs. Thorpe for 30£ sent an order to Thorpes for 16 sacks of SSS flour and 10cwt, of bran and 20cwt of fourths, the snow is all gone, it has been a fine day for the time of year.
Thursday 22nd.	Went to Pilsley in the morning, got Bute shod fore feet, took Mrs Turner. Went to Rowsley in the afternoon with plough to Mr Holmes to have a new share made, took a paraffin oil cask to Rowsley Station, William ploughing a little in the far common piece. Recvd. 3 letters one from Hull one from Mr Travis of the Old Swan and an invoice for some lard from Mancheser, a very cold day.
Friday 23rd.	Thrashing in the morning went to Bakewell in the afternoon, paid Mr Orme for 1 gallon of gin and 2 qrts of wine and all that I bought of him this day. Wm. and Father took the weels off both carts and mixed the chop in the afternoon. Mr Lees called and paid all that he owed me, a frosty day very cold in the morning.
Saturday 24th.	William and I went to Boythorpe for coal for Mr Sculthorpe

took 2 carts and 3 horses, Mr Cocker sent 27¼ lbs of beef and paid for it 18s. Recvd. An invoice from Newark for 16 sacks of flour 20cwt. of fourths and 10cwt, of bran. Recvd. The lard from Manchester, sent the remaining half notes to Newark to complete 30£, a very fine frosty day, the roads very good got home from the coal pit about ½ past 4. Paid John Smith another 1s. for the newspaper this is the

4s. that I have paid him

Sunday 25th.

Christmas Day. Sister Sarah came last night, a very fine day hard frost.

Monday 26th.

Went to Rowsley Station with 2 carts twice and brought the flour &e that I had from Newark, thence I went to Bakewell Market Father and my Mrs and George went with me, Father brought the light cart home whe went to Ashford and stayed untill Tuesday night, Wm. choped a little and looked after the cattle the remainder of the day, a fine frosty day.

Tuesday 27th.

Wm. leading manure in the south field Father looking after the cattle a very fine frosty day.

Wedensday 28th.

Took Mr Deeley some flour thay paid me what thay owed me and for this flour, I sent them 5cwt. of bran brought a paraffin cask from Rowsley Station. Wm. leading manure in the south field, father and I choped some in the afternoon the day is very fine but began to thaw. Went to Wm. Lees at night.

Thursday 29th.

Wm. lead 3 loads of manure then went spreading manure the day out I went to Chatsworth to see Mr Cottingham he told me that the field that whe had the dispute about wanted ploughing so whe must finish ploughing it. Father and I went and mended the fence in the Mains, whe had a party at night, Mr Mayhew and Mrs, and the Mrs sister Miss Stanton and Mr Wm. & J & A Lees and Aunt from Ashover, a very fine day the frost nearly all gone.

Friday 30th.

Wm. went ploughing in the common piece I and Father went with him in the morning, I went to Bakewell in the afternoon Aunt went with me and Miss Stanton whe came back with A Lees. I bought 12qrs. of Oats of Mr Gregory of Meadow Place at 10½ per stone. Mr Thompson of Rowsley is to have 4 or 5 qrs. of them, butter 1s. 5d. per lb, a fine mild day

Saturday 31st.

Wm. ploughing all day Father with him all day, I looked up and mended 16 sacks to send to Mr Gregory to put the oats in, I was looking after the cattle, the singers came at night, gave them 3s. and plenty of drink and some went into Mr Mayhews, I borrowed of him 15£. A fine day began to freeze.

1865

Sunday Jan. 1st.

Took the sheep some oats and bran for the first time, one of the hoggs tuped on the 26th. A fine winterly day, frost and a little snow.

In the margin. Rev. Sculthorpe delivered a most insulting

discourse in the afternoon on neglect of administering the Babtismal [*baptismal*] service.

Monday 2nd.

Got boxer sharpned, Wm. leading manure in the south field I went to Ashford, Father and Charles went with me. Took Peter Furniss wool up and paid him for it 8 tod 18lbs. and 3 lbs locks at 65s.6d. per tod, it began to snow about 2 o'clock and snowed hard untill about 9 at night. Mother came to see us I went to the Hill Top at night stoped till after 5am. Mr and Mrs Mayhew was there.

Tuesday 3rd.

Jobing about and choping some for the horses then oiled part of the gearing, I was jobing about Father came home about 5 pm. A good deal of snow went to Mr Mayhews at night, Alfred was there whe played wist untill one o'clock

Wedensday 4th.

Wm. went to Boythorpe for coal for Mr Spencer with one cart, I and Father and Elizabeth and Sarah finished thrashing what oats there was in the barn, a very roughf wind the snow most of it gone.

Thursday 5th.

Went with Father and Wm. in the far common piece helped them set a ridge then came home. S Pearson came to fetch Sister but it was raining in the afternoon they did not go. I killed a pig, Isaac Grindy helped us a very fat pig too.

Friday 6th.

Wm. went ploughing Father went with him, I looking after the cattle, went to Rowsley to see Mr Thompson when to go to the Meadow Place for the oats, whe arranged for Tuesday next, cut the pig up it weighed 24 stones, began snowing after dinner some very heavy snow storms, Mother and Sister and S Pearson went home, thay left about half past two.

Saturday 7th.

Whe got the last stack in, in the morning, I went with Wm. ploughing in the afternoon helped him set a ridge, then came back and took some flour out then went to Rowsley for one load of the nut slack 8s. per ton brought 14cwt. took the share to the smithey brought a swingletree home that was there. Wm.'s month is up today he talks of leaving he is going to stop a few days or a week untill whe get another.

Sunday 8th.

I did not go to church, I cannot go after being insulted by the clergyman in the Church. A fine mild day.

Monday 9th.

Went to Edensor and Pilsley to Bakewell took J Hawley 20 stone flour, S Norton 20st. Mr Spencer 10st. stoped and dined at the Rutland Arms at the Annual Meeting of the Bakewell Farmers Club. William ploughing Father looking after cattle.

Tuesday 10th.

Went to the Meadow Place for $7\frac{1}{2}$ qrs. of oats at $10\frac{1}{2}$d. per stone. Killed S Halkworth a pig after I got home. Wm. ploughing Father looking after the cattle.

Wedensday 11th. Went with Wm. ploughing in the morning, went to Rowsley in the afternoon got the plough irons and barrow handles mended brought Wm. Downs on load of slack took 2 qrs. of oats to the mill to be ground for the horses. Paid Mr Boden 15s. for 1 ton of coal slack for Wm. Downs.

Thursday 12th. Thrashing in the morning then Wm. went ploughing, whe cleaned up and made ready for choping took the calves to the Lydgets, choped a little at night, very stormy in the afternoon.

Friday 13th. Choped some in the morning then went to the mill for the ground oats, ??? the cows, Went to Bakewell Market in the afternoon Mrs went with me. Recvd. A letter from the Rev G S Outram a very appr. letter too Wm. ploughing Father with him part of the day.

Saturday 14th. Altering the horse gear belonging to the thrashing machine, took Mr Mayhew to Rowsley Station, Wm. shaking straw to two hours in the turnip house choping in the afternoon, went to Mr Sculthorpe at night took his bill, he settled with me.

Sunday 15th. Went to Church in the morning, a wet miserable day.

Monday 16th. Thrashing in the morning paid Wm. his wages 1£ 2s. 6d. he left us, then I went ploughing in the far common piece Father went with me, Frank Staveley took the plough share to the smithy, sent Mr Travis a newspaper, a very fine day. A man from Buxton Station was at Mrs Mayhews he often comes when the master is from home, I cannot understand them I expect there will be a divorce case.

Tuesday 17th. Frances Bottom came and engaged with us at the rate of 17£ for the year until Christmas next if either of us is dissatisfied with each other to give or take either one months wages or one month warning, to come tomorrow Wedensday. I was ploughing in the far common piece, Father with me most of the day and looking after the cattle, a fine day rather frosty.

Wedensday 18th. Went and finished ploughing the far common piece then went coursing in the afternoon. Frank came at noon he cleaned up the yard in the afternoon.

Thursday 19th. Frank ploughing in the bering gate took the young mare Father looking after the cattle, I went to Pilsley in the afternoon took Mr S Hibbert some flour got Short shod, a fine day.

Friday 20th. Gathering some bills got some sacks ready and sent them to Newark, 30 of mine and 18 of Thorpes, sent half notes

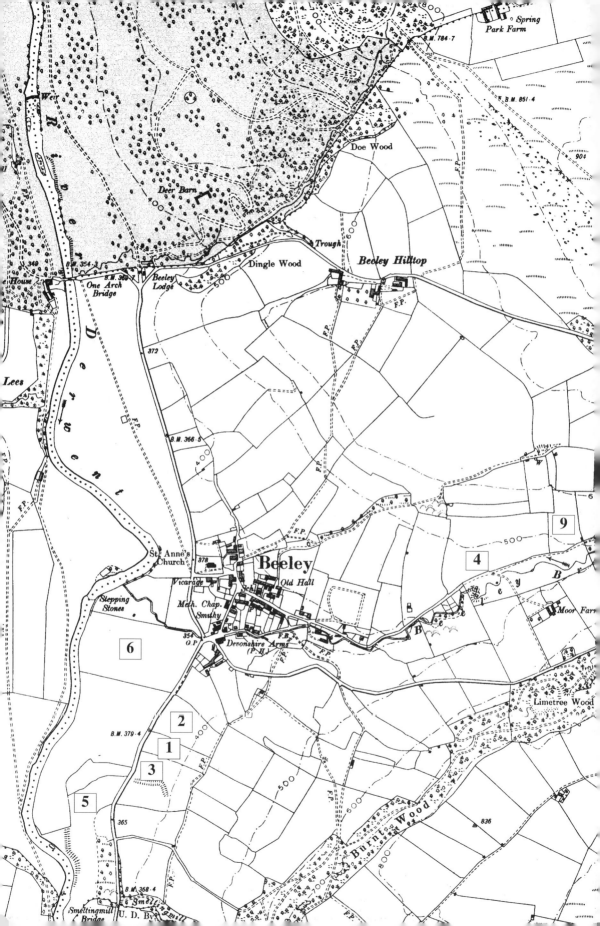

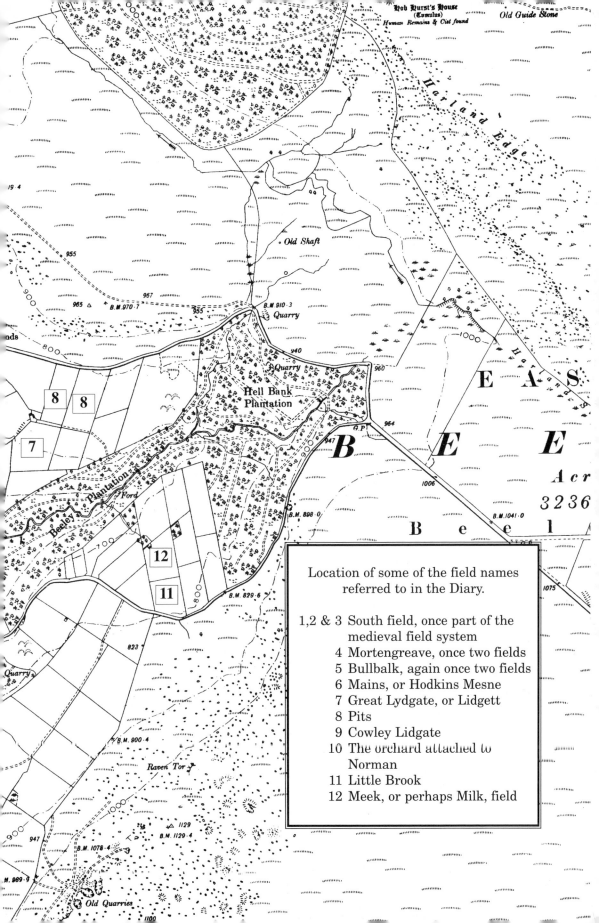

Hob Hurst's House
(Tumulus)
Human Remains & Cist found

Old Guide Stone

Harland Edge

Old Shaft

Quarry

B.M.910·3
Quarry

Hell Bank
Plantation

Quarry

955
965 △ B.M.970·7

800

ads

Beeley Plantation

Ford

8 8

7

12

11

B.M.898·0

B.M.829·6

823

B.M.900·4

Raven Tor

1129
B.M.1129·4

B.M.1078·4

M.989·9

Old Quarries

1100

E A S

B E E

A cr

3236

1006

B.M.1041·0

B e e l

1075

Location of some of the field names
referred to in the Diary.

1,2 & 3 South field, once part of the
medieval field system
4 Mortengreave, once two fields
5 Bullbalk, again once two fields
6 Mains, or Hodkins Mesne
7 Great Lydgate, or Lidgett
8 Pits
9 Cowley Lidgate
10 The orchard attached to
Norman
11 Little Brook
12 Meek, or perhaps Milk, field

to the amount of 35£. Went to Bakewell in the afternoon, Frank went to Bakewell he went and spread some manure in the south field, Father looking after the cattle. I enter three parties in the County Court Martin & Wm. Furniss and Thos. Harrison, John Higingbotham promised to send me what he owed me, a fine day rather frosty.

Saturday 21st. Jobing about most of the day, Frank leading manure in the south field, Father looking after the cattle whe thrashed a little in the afternoon, Lent Mrs Mayhew one bottle of gin. Alfred and Henry Lees came at night Mr Spencer called and stayed a little played a few games at cards, John Lindlam came and paid me what the late Peter Lindlam owed me, a very frosty day.

Sunday 22nd. A fine frosty day.

Monday 23rd. Frank went to Boythorpe for coal for Mr Spencer with one horse, I and Father went to Bakewell Market, I paid T Cocker for 4 loads of lime, Mr Frost of Sheldon paid me for 4 bottles of Annetto, Received prices of flour &e from Newark got Bute shod at Rowsley a fine frosty day.

Tuesday 24th. Frank went to Stoney Middleton with 2 carts for lime I arranged with them to have the lime at 4s 6d per ton, he

'Frank went to Stoney Middleton with 2 carts for lime'
© Derbyshire County Council

brought 17cwt. on one cart and 21 cwt on the other. Sent an order to Newark for 24 sacks of flour and 20cwt. bran 20cwt fourths, sent the remaining ½ notes for 35£, thrashed a little with Short, a fine frosty day.

Wedensday 25th.

Leading slags to Rowsley for Marsden & Co. Frank and I with 2 carts in the morning and 3 carts in the afternoon lead 5ton 9cwt at 2s. 6d. per ton, a fine frosty day

Thursday 26th.

I went to Chesterfield with Short but I could not sell him,

Chesterfield Market Place
© Derbyshire County Council

it was a very bad horse fair, I never had one shilling bid. Frank went to Boythorpe for coal with 2 carts, 15cwt. for Mr Sculthorpe and 17 for Wm. Ludlam. A very rough day it snowed all day, I had a very rough journey from Chesterfield.

Friday 27th.

Recvd. An invoice from Newark for flour 48£ 14s. Recvd. my yearly acct. from Newark I owe them 167£ . Recvd. a letter from Miss M. Wheatley she said that in her late sisters will she leaves to my wife a legacy of 10£ and to my son Albert William she leaves 20£ free from legacy duty. Whe were jobing about thrashing a little choping &e. A very rough day a very deal of snow fell during last night and it snowed most of the day.

Saturday 28th.	Jobing about Frank went to the mill with 2 qrs. of oats for meal and 1 qr. To be split for the horses, whe fetched the old part of the hay that I bought of Mr Outham 2 little loads. Recd. from Mr Walton of Halifax 22£ 12s 9d. being the amount due to me from him for wool that I had paid for, Young Shaw calved and is doing well nice roan cow calf, a fine day but very winterly. Sent Messrs Thorpe & Co. checks for 22£ 12s. 9d. *Note: Seems odd that both amounts of money were the same.*
Sunday 29th.	I went to Ashford to see Alice Aldgate she is a great deal better but very weak, a fine day but very frosty and cold.
Monday 30th.	A good deal more snow fell during last night, Frank and I went twice to Rowsley Station for flour & offals took 2 horses in one cart the roads very heavy so much snow on them. Frank fetched one load of coals for Luke Martin. Killed a pig in the afternoon, Father looking after the cattle, it looks rather like a thaw.
Tuesday 31st.	Leading slags out of Lindup lead 4 tons 16cwt. brought 5 loads of flour and offals home from Rowsley Station that I had from Newark Father looking after the cattle and hung the bacon that was killed one month since, the snow wasting a little, rain and a little snow with it at night.
	In the margin; The pig weighed 18st. 5lbs.
Wedensday 1st.	February. Leading slags to Rowsley Station lead 5ton 9cwt. 2qrs. David Vickers lead 2 tons for us, I am to deduct 5s. off their account brought 11 cwt. of slack from Peter Bailey at 8s. per ton.The snow has wasted a good deal during the day, a little rain at night, Father looking after the cattle.
Thursday 2nd.	Frank went to Middleton for two loads of lime, looking flour & takeing it out, helped Frank to take the lime in the Bering gate the snow continues wasting. Went to Mr Mortimers at night and settled with him for last year, he paid me for 2 tons 5cwt. of bran
Friday 3rd.	Frank went for lime with 2 carts, I took some flour to Pilsley and to Halksworths at lees, brought meal from 1 qr. Oats and 1 qr. Split, the snow still keeps wasting, Old Mr Bentley called to see us.
Saturday 4th.	Frank went to Doythorpe for coal for Mr Spencer 2 tons. I not doing much sent a check to the Paraffin compy. at Birmingham for 3£ 12s. 6d. all that I owe them, sent half notes for 20£ to Messrs Thorpe & Co. of Newark, a very cold day freezes rather sharp again.
Sunday 5th.	A fine frosty day.
Monday 6th.	Took Boxer to the smithy got him shod on the fore feet.

Frank leading manure with 2 horses until I got back, then whe led with 2 carts and three horses least 13 loads, a fine day frosty.

Tuesday 7th.

Fetched one cord of wood out of Lindup for Mr Sculthorpe, then I took Boxer and went to Bakewell with the weights took one sack of fourths to Ashford for D Milnes Father and Frank winnowing some oats in the afternoon, it rained very hard this morning. Sent the rest of the half notes for 20£ to Newark, wrote for 4 hampers of apples, wrote to Mr

Travis, fetched J Halksworth 1 load of coal from Rowsley.

Wedensday 8th. Finished winnowing 3 qrs. of oats sent them to Baslow mill to be made into meal, Frank went forward to the lime kiln to Stoney Middleton for 2 loads of lime. I got the black horse shod on the fore feet. Sent D Milnes 12 gallons of paraffin oil, found one hogg in Mr Ludlams mains another hogg missing I am afraid it is lost, I looked for it but could not find it, frosty again.

Thursday 9th. Took the lime in the hiring gate the black horse whe put in the middle, my mare hath a humour fallen in one of her hind legs, Shenton came and looked at her he gave her one ball and left two more to give her. Took Boxer to Rowsley and got him shod on the fore feet, whe trussed 11$\frac{1}{2}$ cwt. of hay out of Mr Outhams little stack, a frosty day.

Friday 10th. Frank went for 2 tons of coal for Mr Sculthorpe, I went to Bakewell in the afternoon took the young mare. Mr A Lees stoped with us all last night he went with me to Bakewell in the afternoon, I have made inquiry but I cannot hear of the hogg that is missing.

Saturday 11th. Frank went to lime kiln for 2 loads of lime, he brought 20 pks. of meal from Baslow Mill on top of the lime. R Walton brought me 35 pks of apples at 1s. per peck, D Milnes brought me 5 pks of apples and 5 pks of onions, a very frosty day very sharp. Mr Sculthorpe called at night to see us.

Sunday 12th. A very fine frosty day, Frank went home.

Monday 13th. I went to Mr Syburry of Snitterton for some straw for beding, brought 10cwt 1qr. At 3 Guineas per ton. Frank leading slags out of Lyndup to Rowsley Station some snow fell in the morning part, let Mr Southey have one fowl and one ram weighing 22$\frac{1}{4}$ lbs. at 10 d. per lb.. Made Mr Mayhews bill out he did not pay me.

Tuesday 14th. Leading slags out of Lyndup with 2 horses lead in all yesterday and today 9ton 1cwt. for G Marsden & Compy. brought one load of sawdust from Rowsley saw mill at 1s 6d. per load, choped some for horses in the morning, a fine frosty day.

Wedensday 15th. Frank went to the lime kill[n] for 2 loads of lime got the horses sharpened at Pilsley as he wont, took S Norton 1 bag of flour. I went to Chatsworth to borrow the force pump to force the water into our troughf but it is frozen, I could not get the water to come. I was jobing about the remainder of the day, it was late when Frank got home whe did not take the lime in the field, this 2 loads makes 12 loads in all this year in the hiring gate.

Thursday 16th.	Took the two loads of lime in the hiring gate then I went to Rowsley for 1 load of coal for Edward Martin, Frank went to Baslow Mill for the meal off the 5 qrs. of oats that I sent to the mill last week, then whe choped a little after dinner, then whe trussed the last of the hay up that I bought of Mr Outham. S Buxton called and tried to buy one incalf stirk but whe could not agree for the price I offered her for 9£ 10s. he offered me 9£ 5s. for her. Very severe frost last night, rather milder today a good deal of snow is falling tonight.
Friday 17th.	Frank ridled a few hay seeds sawed some stakes, weighed the hay that whe trussed yesterday and several sundry jobs, a good deal of snow is falling.
Saturday 18th.	Jobing about most of the day, I went to Rowsley with some stakes to be sawn they are sawn for 1s 6d. Called at the Peacock Mr Shenton was there I bought a horse of Peter Barlow, Shenton is to do the doctoring after I fetch her for nothing I expect it is only nonsense, a very winterly day
Sunday 19th.	The snow is a good deal of it gone, Mary Evans called and had her tea with us.
Monday 20th.	Went to Bakewell Market I bought 4 pigs of S Hassop for 7£ 10s. or 37s. 6d. each. Borrowed 5£ of Mr Orme , brought the pigs home met Mr Newton of Windmill with Short, sold him for 21£, P Bailey wants me to fetch the mare but I shall not have her. Frank went for coal with 2 carts, one for ourselves and one for S Gardner. A very sharp frost a cold winterly day.
Tuesday 21st.	Mr Holmes stayed with all last night, I ordered 6qrs. oats at 26s. per qrt. And 7qrs of black ones at 1s per stone. Went to Rowsley with Mr Holmes to the Station, I saw Mr Shaw then he would have me to go and see P Bailey and settle about the mare I offered to sink 10s. to be off the bargain. Mr Shaw agreed to take the mare for 11£ 10s. with me sinking 10s. makes up the money 12£ which I was to give him for looking up sacks and mending some and jobing about, Frank lead 4 loads of manure in the mains, he ridled some hay seeds, rather a milder day softened a little.
Wedensday 22nd.	Sent 58 of my sacks and 21 of Thorpes to Newark, fetched one load of stakes and edge wood out of the mill field from the edge that they are staking by Oakley Lane. Frank leading manure in the mains, the wind is got south it thaws a little. H Lees left us 15st. 7lbs. of oats. A person called from Derby wanted me to take an agency for selling superphosphate and grass manure, I promised him that I would write to him about it on Saturday.

Thursday 23rd. Frank and I leading slags to Rowsley Station with two carts, wrote 2 letters one to Thorpes and one to Mr Travis, fine day but very bad roads the snow and all most all gone.

Friday 24th. Frank spreading manure all day I was nocking manure in the forenoon, I went to Bakewell in the afternoon sold the butter at 18d. per lb. Brought some things for Mr Sculthorpe, paid Mr Orme the 5£ which I borrowed on Monday. Mary Evans rode with me part of the way to Bakewell she came back with me. Mr A Lees came from Manchester and stayed with us all night, it continued to thaw.

Saturday 25th. Frank spreading manure, I went to Darley Mill for 24 stones of bean meal (18s. for 16 stones) fetched one load of sawdust from Mr Shaws saw mill, a beautifull fine day for the time of the year. Sent our order to Newark for 2 tons of flour, 8cwt. of sharps, 20cwt. of fourths, 20 sacks of SSS flour, 4 sacks of A flour.

Wrote a letter to the man from Derby that called for me to take an agency to sell manure for a Nottingham firm.

Sunday 26th. Aunt and Elizabeth came from Ashford to see us, I went to the Chappel at night to hear W. Funttons funeral sermon preached.

Monday 27th. Frank spreading manure and nocking in the forenoon, leading manure for Mathew Grindey in the afternoon. I not doing much, took the black [horse] for J Evans to take the drug to Edensor twice he works very nicely. The Mrs rather poorly she is expecting to be confined every hour, Old Betty Stone here all last night and all day today. Very frosty this morning but a fine day.

Note. The 'drug' a waggon used for carrying big timber and tree trunks.

Tuesday 28th. Frank leading manure for Matthw. Grindley in the morning lead 5 loads, whe went ploughing single in the afternoon. J Evans took the black horse in the drug twice, I took him to Rowsley and had him shod a fine day.

Wedensday 1st March. Choping in the morning then Frank and I went ploughing the remainder of the day single in the wood close a fine day except a few showers.

Thursday 2nd. Went to the hoggs found one dead, then I went to Baslow and paid some bills went by Pilsey expecting to have recvd. some money but did not receive one shilling, came to Edensor called at Mr Jepsons and Mr Spencers and then at Mr Mortimers. Bought one pig of Mr Mortimer at 6s. per stn.to come on Monday, Frank ploughing, recvd. an invoice from Newark 10 sacks SSS Flour 4A 8cwt. of sharps 20cwt.

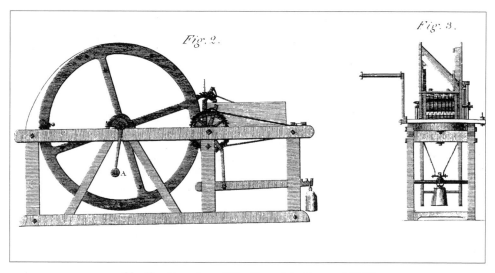

Chaff cutters from 'The Complete Farmer' 1807

	bran 10 cwt. fourths, showery in the morning fine towards night but very windy.
Friday 3rd.	Frank ploughing part of the day, whe fetched 10 sacks 0f SSS flour, 4A 5 Fourths 1 ton bran and 8cwt sharps from Rowsley station. I skinned the hogg that died yesterday. I went to Bakewell in the afternoon came back by the 4 pm train sold butter at 1s 6d per lb. Mr Sculthorpe paid me what I had done for him last week, a fine day.
Saturday 4th.	Frank leading sand with 2 horses for S Downs at 5s. per day each, leading from opposite Chatsworth to Edensor Church. I was jobing about home all day, Father nocking dung at the Lydget. Recvd. a dockument from Messrs. Wheatley lawyer repecting the Legacies 20£ for Albert and 10£ for the Mrs. Signed them and returned them by post to the Lawyer again, very roughf wind began to rain towards night.
Sunday 5th.	A fine day rather cold.
Monday 6th.	Frank leading slags with 2 carts I went with him the first time he went twice and a half. I went to Edensor and Pilsley took some flour, I took the young black horse went forward to Bakewell Market. Paid Mr Jepson for 3 qrs. of malt, paid my subscription to the Bakewell Farmers Club. I ordered 3qrs more malt of Mr Jepson at 56s. per qr. The Mrs very poorly all day she was delivered of a little girl at 45minutes after 3pm. Recvd. a letter from Mr Holmes of Kingsterndale saying that he could not send me the oats that I ordered. Recvd. an account from Thorpes of Newark

for 37£ 16s.3d. A fine day but rather frosty.

In the margin: Bought 2qrts of brandy from Mr Orme.

Tuesday 7th.

Frank leading slags yesterday and today, 9ton 17cwt. 2qrs. I was jobing about killed the pig that I bought of Mr Mortimer, writing several letters and writing several peoples books. Recvd a letter from Miss Wheatleys lawyers repecting the Legacies that Miss Wheatley willed to Albert and my Mrs. frost in the morning but a fine day.

Wedensday 8th.

Frank leading lime to Edensor from Rowsley Station for S Downs, I fetched one load of pea sticks from the top of the Park for the Rev Sculthorpe, cut the pig up that I killed yesterday weighed 30stone 12lbs. paid for it the same time 10£ 5s. 9d. Wrote a letter to Miss M. Wheatley and one to Mr Hunt of Derby. Frosty morning but a fine day.

Thursday 9th.

Frank leading lime and sand for Saml. Downs, I was jobing about most of the day. Recvd. two letters from Thorpes and one from Miss Wheatleys Lawyers saying that they had paid the legacies in the London and Westminster Bank.Frosty in the morning but a fine day. My Mrs. Going on very well considering. I fetched 2 bags of bean meal from Mr Else of Darley Mill.

Friday 10th.

Frank leading sand for S Downs, I jobing about home trussing hay to take to the Lydget for the calves, Father took it at night with Coker? Whe choped some with Chance and Bute, a very roughf wind, very sharp frost in the morning, the Mrs going on very well. Mrs Mortimer called to see the Mrs, I made the acct. out for leading stone to the Highways last year 4£17s6d.

Saturday 11th.

Frank leading sand for S Downs, I was gardening most of the day, Frank fetched one load of sawdust from Rowsley Saw Mill. Blackman cow calved a bull calf. I received a letter for Miss Wheatley, one from Mr Spencer he wants one load of coals. A very roughf wind and cold day My Mrs got up for a few hours towards night she seems to be going on very well.

Sunday 12th.

A fine day and not so cold as it was yesterday. Mrs came down into the parlour to her tea she stayed there untill 8 o'clock then she went to bed. Old Shaw calved bull calf. Matth. Martin came to Beeley at night he had walked 41 miles, came from Halifax this morning.rode part of the way.

Monday 13th.

Frank went ploughing the fallow in the Bering gate, I went with him and took the black hors[e] in the afternooon, I was pruning the goosberry trees in the morning, Joseph Morley called and bought the 2 bull calves to go on

Thursday for 2£ and 2 s 6d returned. The Mrs in the parlour most of the day she seems very well considering, a fine day, called at Mr Worralls about the soil being removed that they have taken off the road up to the wood close and bering gate. He promised me he would see Mr Cottingham about it.

Tuesday 14th.

Frank ploughing all day, I fetched 2 loads of flour and offals from Rowsley station. Wrote 2 letters one ordering 10qrs of oats and 5qrs of oats and 3qrs. of beans as per sample of Mr Heighton of Nottinham, the 10qrs 24s. the 5 qrs. 26s.6d beans 40s per qr. Sent an order to the Nottingham Mills Company for 2 tons of superphosphate to me at Nottingham 6£ 10s per ton, a fine day.

Wedensday 15th.

Frank fetched one load of coals for Mr Spencer of Edensor, I fetched the remainder of the flour and offals from Rowsley 10 bags SSS flour at 31s. 10 cwt. 6s 6d. 15 cwt. bran 5s 6d. 5 cwt. at 5s. total 24£ 2s 6d. Then I went to Mrs Frosts sale at Baslow I bought 4 rakes and 2 heads for 8d. one tureen? 3d. one straw stack 5£, sold the straw stack for 5£ 2s 6d. to Mr Furniss of Longstone. A very fine day for the time of year rather a cold wind.

Thursday 16th.

Frank ploughing all day in the fallow, I took one load of lime from Rowsley to Edensor Church for S Downs, looking up sacks and sending them off to Newark 17 of Thorpes and 28 of mine to be filled with oats for seed. J Mosley fetched the 2 bull calves, I bought one cow calf of Cardwell for 25s. I set the old goose yesterday with 11 eggs. A very fine day rather cold.

Friday 17th.

Frank leading two loads of lime to Edensor and fetched 2 more and put them in the cart shed he went ploughing in the afternoon. I went to Bakewell in the afternoon drawed Albert and my Mrs legacies out of the Bakewell Bank 30£ in all, Albert 20£ and the Mrs 10£. I took 7½ lbs. butter sold it at 16½d. per lb. She did not pay me for it, I took 3 score eggs sold them at 18 for 1s. I set one row of peas and one row of beans after I got home. Mary Evans came and paid 19s. for the sheep that Miss Waltons dog ran into the Derwent and she paid for 1 leaf fat, a fine day.

Saturday 18th.

I took the 2 loads of lime to Edensor with Bute, brought John Halksworth one load of manure from Edensor, Father took some hay to the Lydget for the calves, Frank ploughing all day with the black horse and Boxer. I gardened a bit set another row of beans and made the bed ready for shalots. Recvd. an invoice from Mr Heighton for the oats and beans 24£ 12s 6d. A fine day but bitter cold wind.

Sunday 19th.	Drabble calved about 2 o'clock in the morning nearly a red cow calf, A bitter cold day North East wind.
Monday 20th.	Frank and I leading slags and brought 4 loads of oats and beans from the station, 15 qrs. from Nottingham and 3qrs. beans. Mr Ludlam had 10 qrs. of them I took 3 sacks of beans and 2qrs. of the oats that came from Nottingham to the Mill, 14 qrs. came from Newark brought 10 of them home, left 4 at the station. I recd. the invoice from Newark 17£ 16s 4d. the oats. Recvd. A receipt for 30£ which I sent to Thorpes on Friday last. The little heifer calved not made much bag a nice roan cow calf a little one. A very cold day very frosty, Father went to Bakewell Market.
Tuesday 21st.	Frank leading manure in the forenoon, I took 2 loads of slags to Rowsley Station with boxer, choped a little, Frank fetched 2 loads of slags out of Lyndup in the afternoon to Rowsley, got boxer shod of 3 feet bute of one foot. Got some pea sticks out of the smelting Mill plantation, Frank brought them home, a very cold wind very frosty, paid the carriage of the oats and beans from Nottingham16s. sack hire 1s 6d. The calves is very bad of the scour the one that I bought, Drabbles and the heifers. Mr Lees came at night and paid his bill up to this date.
Wedensday 22nd.	Frank fetched one load of coals from Boythorpe then whe fetched 2 loads of lime from Rowsley ready for the morning. I went to Whitworths for some hay for Mr Grindy but they had none trusted and was buisy with all the men so I came back without any. I got a piece of iron put on the old cart to hold it together. Joseph Froggatt called, Gregory calved in the morning a cow calf nearly a red one, the other three calves no better of the gir? Cold day again Mr Deeley paid me his bill.
Thursday 23rd.	Frank leading sand with boxer and Captain for S Downs, Father and I winnowing the last of the oats, a frosty day and rather cold a few snowstorms,
Friday 24th.	Frank leading manure into the mains all day with one horse. I went to Whitworths of Darley for one half of the hay for Mr Grindey, the two calves died this morning, I skinned them and took the skins to Bakewell, sold them to Mr Thompson for 3s.3d. took the light cart and Bute took Mr Clay 2qrs. of oats he paid me 1£ 5s. per qr. for things, took Richard Frost 3 bottles of annetto, sold 15lbs. of butter at 16d per lb. Recd. 10s 5d. for 7½lb last weeks butter. Brought new scales from Wallises 8s. Brought some things for Mr Sculthorpe, Drabbles calf and the little heifers died. Made the first cheese today this years. Frosty weather yet, very cold wind. Young Shaw buld by the Dukes bull.

Saturday 25th.	Frank went to Boythorpe for 1 ton of coal for Mr Sculthorpe, choped a little jobing about most of the day, fetched one load of sawdust from the saw mill at Rowsley. Snow and frost barometer very low.
Sunday 26th.	Cold North wind and some heavy snow storms.
Monday 27th.	Frank leading manure in the forenoon, I went to Darley ordered half a ton of hay of Mr Whitworth, called at Mr Else and paid him all I owe him 13£ 7s. I ordered 9 sacks of flour of him at 1s 6d. per stone and he sent it in the afternoon, S Buxton called I sold him 3 stirks for 25£ to be drawn some time this week Mr Wain came and stayed with us about one hour. Rosy calved a white cow calf, made the second cheese today. Father went to the Bakewell Union then he went forward to Ashford, went to a meeting of the members of the Cow Club at night. Frank leading lime for S Downs in the afternoon with two horses, took a bit of hay to the Lydget for the calves, a fine day rather frosty at night, took Mr Sculthorpe 1 load of manure
Tuesday 28th.	I went to Mr Whitworths for some hay 12½ cwt. at 6£ 6s. per ton, 3£ 18s 8d. took most of it to the Lydget for the calves. Saml. Buxton sold the stirks again today to Mr Archer of Meadow Place for 25£ 15s. he is to send for them tomorrow. Frank leading lime for S Downs. Bute is very lame of one hind foot, The first ewe lambed 2 lambs, milder weather a very fine day.
Wedensday. 29th.	Frank ploughing with Captain and Boxer, I shot the oats and beans and sent 44 sacks, railway sacks back to the station by Livy Stone. G Merhill putting spouting up on the back of the cowhouse, thay put us a new pipe end on to bring the water in the yard. The white calf hath begun of the gir? I gave it this morning two teaspoonsfull of laudnum and one tablespoonful of tincture of rubarb, to night I gave it one good dose of Lulingtons Medicine, it seems very bad, a nice mild day mild tonight.
Thursday 30th.	Frank and I moving the soil thay have taken off the road up to the wood close and the bering gate, Robt. Halksworth and Jim Downs filling the soil. 4 sheep lambed today one lambed before whe got up it died was very weakly, the other 3 had 4 strong lambs all doing well, a very fine day, the white is very bad of the gir? I gave it 2 more doses of Lulingtons medicine
Friday 31st.	Whe went sowing oats in the far common piece, I sowed rather more than 3 sacks of the oats that is not as good colour I had them from Nottingham, up the side of the field; Father gathering stone with Captain in the morning then he was righting sods and rakeing places that was not

covered. I went to Bakewell in the afternoon, another sheep lambed one lamb, the wite calf still very bad I gave it some soot in its milk this morning and two eggs, tonight I gave it burnt flour and then I gave it some earning? in a little milk. Artington will calve tonight I think she is very uneasy, a very fine day mild spring weather but the ground is very dead not a bit of grass to be seen. I wrote a letter to Mr Outram yesterday .

Saturday 1st April. Artington calved early this morning a red and wite cow calf, sowing oats in the far common piece I sowed the remainder of the oats that came from Nottingham, 3qrs. in all. I sowed 1 qr. and 1 strike that came from Newark, the wite calf it is better, whe harrowed with three horses, another sheep lambed one lamb making 9 lambs, a very fine day.

Sunday 2nd. Another sheep lambed 2 lambs, she will not take to one of them another is not well. Artingtons calf very bad of the gir, another fine spring day.

Monday 3rd. 2 more sheep lambed 3 lambs, the 2 lambs very awkward that will not suck, Artingtons calf very bad I gave it soot and 2 eggs, whe sowed 2½ qrs. of oats and one strike, harrowed with 3 horses 1½ qrs. 1 strike that came from Newark thay go to the furrow this side the water trough, the other side was our own grown. T. Harrison was righting sods after whe had harrowed a very fine day rather colder at night East wind. I got a letter from Mr Outram, took several lots of flour out.

Tuesday 4th. Finished sowing the far common piece sowed rather more than 3 sacks. Father righting sods, a very fine day. Sent half notes to Thorpes of Newark for 50£. Sowed in all in the common piece rather more than 8 qrs. 3qrs. of the oats not a good colour, 2½ qrs. from Newark and a little more than 2½ qrs. of our own growth.

Wedensday 5th. The heifer calved a bull calf, frank finished ploughing the wood close, sowed 2 qrs. of oats in the afternoon in the wood close. One lamb died this morning leave us with 14 lambs, whe have put the lamb that the ewe would not take to the one that lost its lamb. Father and I went to Mr Mayhews to dinner at night, a little rain but a beautifull tine day.

Thursday 6th. Finished sowing the wood close then Frank ploughing the turnip ground in the hiring gate. Henry took the plough share to the smithy then he went with me for the 10 hoggs to Eyam paid 4£10s. for their wintering, not grown very well, got home about 8 o'clock at night. James Stone spreading the dirt or soil that came off the road up the bering gate, a fine day rather windy. Sold S Buxton the in-calf stirk for 10 guineas.

Friday 7th.

Frank ploughing all day in the bering gate. I took 24 bushels of malt to Chatsworth and 36 lbs. of hops for the Dukes mowers and 4 strike of malt and 6lbs. of hops for Mr Worrall. I went to Bakewell in the afternoon went to Ashford and Mr Potts went with me. Bought D Milnes hoggs at 42s. each for Mr Potter. Bought Mr Buckleys 3 hoggs for Mr Potter at 35s. each. Sent the remaining half notes to complete the 50£ for Messrs. Thorpe of Newark, took some cloth for Clark to make up for Henry. 4 sheep lambed 5 lambs today the white bull calf died this morning, Artingtons calf very bad of the gir. Whe have 15 sheep lambed and 19 lambs living in all, 6 more to lamb. Alice Aldgate came to stop with us a wile. Recvd. of D Milnes 2£ 5s. being what thay owe me, a very beautifull fine day .

Saturday 8th.

Frank leading slags to Rowsley Station, I finished ploughing the corners and the headlands in the bering gate, whe finished sowing after he had took 5 tons of slags to Rowsley . Artingtons calf is better, a very hot day. Another sheep lambed one lamb making 20 lambs in all. Isaac Grindey brought me a newspaper from Manchester.

Sunday 9th.

A fine hot day thunder and lightning at night very heavy. Mr Mayhew and Mrs went with me to the Lydgate at night.

Monday 10th.

Borrowed a cart and cart saddle of Mr Grafton Frank and I took 3 horses and 3 carts slag leading, lead 7ton 15cwt. Wrote one letter to Mr Potter to say that he may have the stirk that Buxton bought, he not having feetched it, wrote an order for 12 SSS, 8 SS,4A, 2XX flour, 20cwt. of fourths and the remainder to be filled with bran. Ground another sack of malt for the Dukes mowers and let them have 6lbs. of hops, a fine day rather cooler air than yesterday.

Tuesday 11th.

I was leading slags out of Lyndup with 2 horses, Frank went to Boythorpe for 1 ton of coals for Mr Spencer. Jillett calved a very nice cow calf. A very hot day very much like thunder. Made Mr Outhams acct. that I have paid for him and sent him the ballance 2£ 15s 8d. sent them one couple of rabbits allso.

Wedensday 12th

I went to Chatsworth for 25 strike of grains. Brought Fearn 6 strike and Wm. Brown 6 strike. Frank fetched one load of slags out of Lyndup then he went harrowing in the afternoon with the heavy harrow on the potatoe ground. I went to Pilsley with some flower and Mr Spencer some. Brought the heavy harrow Mr Holmes made it, I ordered a new cart body of Mr Holmes. I set the shalots and made the onion bed ready. Sold G Wilson the cow calf that came of Jillett for 24s. A deal of thunder and lightning and some very heavy rain, another sheep lambed one lamb making 21 lambs. I got Boxer shod of the forefeet. I saw Mr Jones about Mr Outhams donkey asked him 25s. for her, he was to satisfy me in a few days if he was to have her.

Thursday 13th. Frank leading manure into the mains James Stone spreading manure J Harper spreading dropings. I borrowed the Dukes chain harrow off Mr Worrall and broke up the manure in the mains, Father leveled and raked the straw up, Frank brought it home, I went to Bakewell in the afternoon worked the chain harrow untill 7 o'clock after I got back from Bakewell. Jilletts calf began of the gir. Fetched 7 goslings in found 1 dead 3 more chiped, a very hot beautifull growing day. Recd. an invoice from Thorpes for flour &e 12 bags SSS, 8SS, 4A, 2 XX, 12 cwt. fourth, 18cwt bran total 48£ 17s.

Good Friday. 14th. Sowed onions lettuce mustard cress radish and set 3 rows of potatose. Choped all the hay up for the cows and gave them some mixed with bean meal and grains, choped some for the horses, hung the bacon that I bought of Mr Mortimer, brought 2 more goslings in one rather weakly, a good deal colder towards night.

Saturday 15th. Frank leading manure in the mains in the morning, rowling the bottom end in the afternoon. James Stone spreading manure and gathering stones in the mains. I fetched one load of sawdust from Rowsley saw mill then fetched 12 SSS. 4A, 2XX sacks of flour, 144st. fourths and 18cwt of bran from Rowsley station. Turned the 9 goslings to the goose, sold G Wilson the stirk for 11£ to go on Monday 24th of the month a very fine day very hot in the afternoon.

Sunday 16th. A very hot day another sheep lambed making 22 lambs 3 more sheep to lamb. D Milnes his wife and Emma Mills came.

Monday 17th. I and Father went to Bakewell Fair Frank harrowing the fallow George Marsden paid me for the slag leading 3£ 16s. Two more sheep lambed one lamb each making 24 lambs in all a good deal of rain last night and a deal of rain this afternoon, beautifull growing day. Father got very drunk he was quite helpless. Paid Mr Sybery for ½ ton straw 1£ 12s 3d.

Tuesday 18th. Frank went to Boythorpe for 2 tons of coal one for ourselves and one for Rev Sculthorpe, I borrowed the Dukes chain harrow and harrowed the manure in the south field and some in the mains. Joseph Harper gathering stones and the straw that the harrow had puled together and Father helping him, Mr Henry Lees married today dined at the Grouse Inn Darley Dale, a very fine warm growing day, J Wilson fetched the cow calf.

Wedensday 19th.

Frank fetched one load of coal from Holymoorside with 2 horses then him and Father raked up and led the straw of the owler greave, I went to the Stand for one load of bracking, a very fine warm day beautiful growing weather.

Thursday 20th.

Frank leading gravel for the Rev. Sculthorpe, I was jobing about, went to Rowsley got a piece of wood sawn at the saw mill paid 3s. for it spending for the rowler shafts. Frank Staveley put them in. Gathering stone in the afternoon Father and Henry and George allso, a very fine day never saw the grass grow so fast, my Mrs went to Ashford. A man came from Matlock and bought the butter at and eggs, the butter at 13½d and the eggs at 18 for 1s. He wanted to contract for one year but whe could not agree, the last sheep lambed one lamb making 25 lambs, [*blank*] ewes, and [*blank*] tup lambs.

Friday 21st.

Frank rowled the south field and the wood close, I and Erbut Buckley Father and Henry finished gathering stones in the south field, Erbut and Henry knocked the dropings in the bull balk and cow close. I went to Ashford for the Mrs at night bought one gallon of gin from Ormes, paid Mr Orme for ½ gallon brandy. John Holmes came and paid his Mothers bill, rather colder wind.

Saturday 22nd.

Frank rowled the far common piece I was edgeing in the meek field the forenoon, Erbut Buckley and Henry nocking dung at Lydget, I went to Pilsley in the afternoon and got a plate put on the light cart shaft got Bute shod on two feet. Took Frank Hawley and Mrs Turner 1 sack of flour each, Colder North East wind very drying. Mrs Travis was intered this day at Edensor aged 26 years.

Sunday 23rd.

Very hot in the middle of the day, but very cold North East wind at night. The young goose hatching 11 eggs chiped.

Monday 24th.

The old goose trod 2 young ones to death she hatched 9 goslings some of them very weakly, turned 5 with her the others whe have in the house, G Wilson fetched the stirk that he bought of me. Frank draging the potato ground and harrowing, he lead 4 loads of manure, Henry and Erbut Buckley finished nocking dung at the Lydget, James Stone rakeing up the straw in the Mains and gathering stones untill noon, the rest all went setting potatose set 8 pecks old ones and about 3 pecks early ones. I cut the lambs tails and belted some of the ewes, turned 4 ewes and

4 lambs into the churchyard. Thomas Elliot paid for 2½ qrs of oats 3£ 7s 6d. Mr Travis called at night, a fine day very cold wind at night very dry.

Tuesday 25th.

Frank rowling and harrowing the hiring gate took 4 loads of manure into the wood close for potatose, James Stone Erbut Buckley Henry and Father and I finished setting potatose, a very fine day very hot, wind got South. Beny Halksworth grafted 1 cherry tree and 6 plumb trees, gave Alfred Lees 2£ for him to pay for some lard, thay brought 14 bags of manure from the Station from Mr Vickers of Manchester 8£ 8s.

Wedensday 26th.

Frank harrowing in the morning, began ploughing in the afternoon. I sent 10 of my sacks and 21 of Thorpes to Newark, gathered 3 loads of stone off the fallow in the afternoon, went to Edensor Mill at night for bean meal of 1 qr beans. Erbut Buckley and Father and Henry gathering twitch, thay was in the flower garden in the morning 2 hours, a very fine day. It is reported that President Lincoln is assassinated shot through the head. *Note: This was 11 days after the event.*

Thursday 27th.

Frank ploughing in the fallow, Father and Henry and Erbut Buckley gathering twitch and stones, I was leading rails and coal for Mr Drabble, Alfred Lees brought me some lard from Manchester in two mugs, I ordered some hay of Squire Thornhill, a very fine day rather looks like rain.

Friday 28th.

Frank ploughing in the fallow, Father, Henry, Erbut Buckley finished gathering twitch, gathered some stones in the mains. I was leading rails and coal for Mr Drabble in the forenoon, fetched 15 cwt. of hay from Mr Thornhill of Stanton $£ 10s. I paid for it, wind got North East, very uncommon cold in the afternoon, sent an order for 12 sacks of flour & 1 ton of bran 1 ton of fourths to Newark.

Saturday 29th.

Leading wood and coal for Mr Drabble, brought one load of sawdust from the top of the Park took Mr Lees some flour, went to Baslow mill for 39 packets malt. Frank ploughing with 2 horses a very fine day but cold wind inclined for frost tonight.

Sunday 30th.

Dry and very cold wind barometer falling. Miss Worrall went to Manchester to Isaac Grindey it is expected thay are [to] get married.

MAY – NOVEMBER 1865

In this period we read of the continuation of the work on rebuilding the Church at Edensor, to the design of Sir George Gilbert Scott. William seems to have been responsible for carting the sand and lime for Mr Downs the builder.

Undoubtedly the highlight of the month of June for much of the surrounding area, was the Great Review in Chatsworth Park. William gives but a brief mention of the event, and I have been fortunate in obtaining a quote from the diary of the 7th. Duke, and a longer and different account from The Derbyshire Times.

Later in the month we read of, "Domney riding up the wall sides," I can't believe that William was paying his man to ride around on a horse, and I have been unable to find an explanation.

Hay making, like corn harvest later in the period, seems to have been a communal affair with everyone helping each other. Perhaps the supply of home brewed beer had something to do with it!

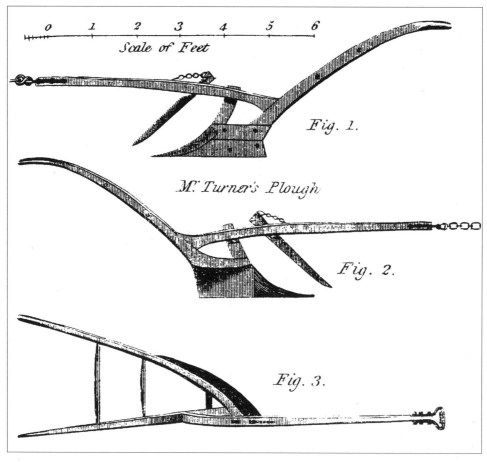

0   1   2   3   4   5   6

Scale of Feet

Fig. 1.

M.ʳ Turner's Plough

Fig. 2.

Fig. 3.

Agricultural machinery
from John Farey's 'Agriculture and Minerals of Derbyshire' Volume two

Monday 1 May.	I gathered in some money in the morning, then went to Bakewell Market, Paid John White for 3 qrs. of oats 3£ 18s. Bought 2 pigs at 28s. each, Killed Mr Buckley one little pig, Saml. Grafton came for some malt and paid their bill. Frank ploughing in the fallow a very fine day inclined for some rain. Recd. an invoice from Newark 12 sacks flour 10 bags fourths 20cwt. bran 30£.
Tuesday 2nd.	Frank finished ploughing the fallow, I lead some wood and some coal for Mr Drabble, some nice rain fell in the afternoon sent 30£ to Thorpes of Newark half notes, sent Mr Outram a newspaper.
Wedensday 3rd.	I fetched some coal from the station then I went to Frank spreading lime it began to rain and stoped us. Whe fetched the bran and flour and fourths from the station. I got Bute shod and the strut stave mended, a good deal of rain fell

towards night.

Thursday 4th.	I sowed 4 bags of fertilizer in the mains, went with John Cocker to the Lydget he looked at the tup and one barren ewe he bid 7d. per lb. for them, I offered them at 7^1/4d. Mr Thompson came and looked at the lambs but thay wernt quite big enoughf. Frank got the ashes out of the ash place and weeled most of them out, went to Edensor in the afternoon for Mr Spencers ashes 2 loads took Halksworth 1 sack of flour a very fine day after the rain. Sent the remaining half notes to Newark 30£
Friday 5th.	Turned the milk cows out into the Mortin greave and pits, Frank finished wheeling the ashes out, he took the black horse to the smithy, took 3 loads of ashes to the top of the wood close ready for the fallow. I was jobing about most of the day, got Mrs Mayhew home in our light cart drove up to Baslow then to Edensor and home again. I went to the Hill Top at night with Mr Mayhew, Mr Lees paid me a bill 15s. for sundries a beautifull growing day a good deal of rain fell during the day.
Saturday 6th.	Frank lead 4 loads of stone from the Lydget to the top of the Mortin to wall the gatestead up then whe all helped to load Mr Mayhews goods and took them to Baslow with the wagon and 2 horses, Frank lead the young horse I took the wagon, a fine growing day.
Sunday 7th.	A very fine day no service at the Church.
Monday 8th.	I and Father and Frank spreading lime in the Bering gate 2 carts and 3 horses finished spreading the lime, took some flour for Wm. Roose fetched the sheep out of the Churchyard put them in the croft, left the milk cows lie out on Saturday night the first time, a very fine day.
Tuesday 9th.	Choped some; I and Father gathered stones in the mains, Frank rowled the top end a good deal of rain fell during the the day, I fetched the tup and one barren ewe from the Lydget Wm. Tomlinson called and looked at them he bid 7^1/4d per lb. I offered them at 7^3/4d. per lb. He would not give it, I turned them in the croft after I had washed them I washed them in a pit.
Wedensday 10th.	I lead 2 tons 7cwt. of slags to Rowsley Station, Father rowled the great Lydget with bute, I turned the 4 ewes and lambs the tup and barren ewe in the Churchyard. I paid Frank his wages 5£ 4s. he left; John Oxspring took the pigs that he bought and paid 16£ 12s 6d. Mr Wilson paid me for the stirk 11£ and the calf that bought 1£ 5s. I gave him 4d. for luck for both, I got 2 pairs of shears ground and set and paid for them 6d. a cloudy day very cold wind.

Thursday 11th.	I slag leading with both horses Father jobing about began to rain at night a fine growing day.
Friday 12th.	I took the sheep out of the mains put them in the mortin greave and put the milk beasts in the cow close and 4 ewea and 4 lambs and the tup and the barren ewe. Then Father and I fenced round the bull balk I fetched J Halksworth 1 load of coals from Mr Boden 12s. per ton. I killed Math. Grindey a pig last night and cut it up this afternoon I sharpened some stakes, rained all day.
Saturday 13th.	Took two loads of wood to Rowsley Station for Mr Drabble had bute hanged up at the station, Henry and George took 3 roan calves on Calton. I took the black horse after dinner he fell on the road between the Church and the Blue doors broke both his knees and hurt my leg he trod on me. 3 cows were bulling I fetched a little bull of J Wilson and turned to them at night, I do not know wether he bulled any of them or not, young Shaw Blackmore and Drabble were bulling lent J Wilson 1£. John Smith brought us an iron bedstead paid for it 1£16s 6d. Sold John Cocker the tup and the barren ewe at 7¹/2d per lb. To go in cours[e] of two or three weeks. A fine day after rain, Mr Lees called at night to see us.
Sunday 14th.	A fine day I and A Lees went to Baslow to see Mr Mayhew, I went to Church in the morning.
Monday 15th.	I went to Bakewell Market Father went too I bought 10 pigs at 28s each let Math. Grindey have 2 at 28s 6d. each Thos Roose one at 28s 6d, a little rain towards night.
Tuesday 16th.	I fetched one load of sawdust and one load of wood from the top of the park paid for them 3s 6d. I fetched 2 loads of slags out of Lyndup, I began to join Mr Sculthorpe at the newspaper yesterday, a very fine day Father mowed nettles in the orchard and the croft a very fine day. I went to the Park at night shooting jackdaws, G Wilson paid me the 1£ that I lent him.
Wedensday 17th.	Took the slags to the Station 2ton 14cwt. then I went to the top of the Park for rails for Mr Drabble to them to the Station, I went harrowing in the fallow in the afternoon Father gathered some stone in the Cowley Lydget and he went spreading some bits of lime that was not fallen when whe spread it. A very fine day had 2 bags of bean meal from Mr Else.
Thursday 18th.	Harrowing in the forenoon washing sheep in the afternoon a very fine day Father belted some of the sheep and made up the sheep wash in the morning
Friday 19th	Harrowing in the fallow in the morning, I went to Edensor

and paid the rent in the afternoon borrowed 1£ of G Wilson called at Mr Spencers and looked round the New Church thay are building got home about 5pm a very fine day S Ludlam paid me for 10qrs. of oats.

The new church being at Edensor.

Saturday 20th.	Harrowing and dragging the fallow all day a very hot day
Sunday 21st.	A very hot day.
Monday 22nd.	Spike rooling the fallow till it began to rain, I fetched one load of stakes? From the top of the Park for Jacob Towndrow, Alice Aldgate came at night Elizabeth began to sleep at Betty Stones, a very fine growing day.
Tuesday 23rd.	Went to Edensor in the morning then I went with 2 horses and took Mr Lees one waggon load of goods to Ashover, Jillett buld a very fine growing day a little rain some thunder and lightning.
Wednesday 24th.	Finished spike rooling the fallow then I went to Mr Deeley with some flower got boxer shod and bute removed on one hind foot. John Mitchell came he helped me, then he went to Mr Deeley and engaged with him a very fine day.
Thursday 25th.	Harrowed the fallow in the forenoon took one load of manure with me, fetched one load of wood in the afternoon, a very fine growing day.
Friday 26th.	Fetched one load of coals from Boythorpe for Mr Spencer. Father opening the soughf that brings the water in the farm yard, another very hot growing day, artington buld.
Saturday 27th.	Fetched two loads of wood from the top of the Park one for G Holmes and the other for Henry Hibbert, paid the sawyer for 4 loads 10s. Father sticking peas and jobing about, John White called for some sacks that I had of his with oats in, I found him 3 all that is come at present 2 more at the mill and one at Mr Mayhew. A very fine hot growing day.
Sunday 28th.	Some nice rain fell in the night and some slight showers during the day
Monday 29th.	I righted some books in the morning then I went to Bakewell Market, paid Mr Else one bill 13£ 10s. Mr Cocker fetched 2 sheep and killed them Father clipped them before he took them, thay weighed 160lbs. at 7$\frac{1}{2}$d per lb. 5£. A very fine day a little rain.
Tuesday 30th.	I lead 5 loads of manure in the hiring gate and ploughed a great piece for rape. I clipped 5 sheep at night one was Mrs Mayhews its fleece weighed 6$\frac{1}{2}$lb, a fine day but roughf wind.
Wedensday 31st.	Finished ploughing the piece I had set out then I sowed 5

95

bags of manure on it, Father sowed part of it with rape he sowed 5lbs of seed then he rowled all he had sowed. H Lees came and whe finished clipping sheep 9 tod 20lbs of wool. Sarah went to Bakewell and brought 3lbs more rape seed and 2lbs pitch, a fine day rather cold wind.

Thursday 1st June. I went to the Hill Top cliping sheep whe finished cliping all Mr Lees, Father sowed the bit that was ploughed with rape and rowled it, Mr Thompson fetched 6 lambs paid 28s. each, a fine day but rather cold looks like rain.

Friday 2nd. A very rainy day fetched one load of nut slack from P Bailey, sent 2 bundles sacks to Newark wrote 3 letters, one to Thorpes one to Mr Walton and one to Sister Sarah.

Saturday 3rd. Leading wood for Mr Drabble and ½ ton coal, a fine growing day Father weeding the corn in the hiring gate.

Sunday 4th. A fine day Brother in law came at night, S Pearson.

Monday 5th. Winster Fair Father and I and S Pearson went to the Fair got home again about 4 o'clock, a very good growing day. G Wilson took his bull to the fair and sold him.

'Winster Fair. Father and I and S Pearson went.'
© Derbyshire County Council

Tuesday 6th. Ploughing some and sowing rape sowed about an acre. Sent ½ notes for 20£ to Newark, a fine growing day turned the cows in the Bull Balk yesterday.

Wedensday 7th. Took 18 sheep and 3 stirks and the donkey in the little brook took 6 sheep that I had sold the lambs off to the Lydget, then whe all went to the great review in Chatsworth Park, I was waiting in one of Jepsons tents took 12£ 8s 6d. A very hot day.

Note: Quoted from the diary of the 7th Duke of Devonshire about the Chatsworth Review. "We had a field day here today of the Derbyshire Yeomanry and Volunteers. Unfortunately owing to delays on the railway the proceedings did not begin till after 2 nearly 2 hours later than was intended- however with this exception, all went off perfectly. The day was splendid & we had a vast number of spectators. The Volunteers & Yeomanry both did extremely well & the sight was really well worth seeing. We had a large number of the country gentlemen etc to lunch. The Colvilles went away at the close of the review".
Presumably, "The waiting in one of Jepsons tents" refers to one of the refreshment tents.

The Great Review in Chatsworth Park 7 June 1865 from a contemporary engraving
© Derbyshire County Council

The Derbyshire Times.
Volunteer and Yeomanry Review
At Chatsworth Park.
7th June 1865.

Wednesday last will long be remembered in Chesterfield and neighbourhood as an eventful day to those who were bent on a visit to Chatsworth Park. From an early hour in the morning everything in the shape of a travelling animal was in request and hundreds others could have been found work if they had been in existence. Suffice it to state that the most grotesque appearances were displayed long prior to getting on the road. We found on entering the Market place as early as 6 o'clock, numbers of holiday attired females, waiting for the waggon or other conveyances which they felt themselves lucky in having chartered some days previously. We always feel amused at a description of a Derby Day, but we think we were little short of having as many unique and amusing scenes and styles of conveyances. There was the old heavy cart horse with his similarly concientious loading-up, viz., licensed to carry 14 in a one horse cart-pace no object, even up Wadshelf Hill, there we viewed the drays loaded with living freights seated on forms, followed by every carriers wagon to be found. When we left the town it appeared as if our tradesmen and gentry had taken leave of everything like business- the shops closed and all bent on the only object of the day. As we observe every style of structure in vehicle was brought into requisition in conveying not only the living occupants but a plentiful supply of the needful to keep them living, We could not but notice the absence of all gauge to the stomach- for instance where the party came to grief near Robin Hood, they consisted of some six or seven in a light cart and on it's shafts giving way, we had exhibited to our view a stock of beef and other eatables which enbued us with the idea that they were out for a week's encampment. Not so- they judged that the air of Chatsworth would have an effect on the stomach, and sure enough it must have if the stock was consumed. The continued line of carriages was a sight worth seeing, even for so short a distance on the road, yet when we arrived at Baslow this village was literally bombarded, for the number of omnibuses was enormous as well as the carriages- but on arrival at the intended review ground, one continued round of conveyances lined the baracaded ground in three and four deep, where the attentions of the county police was in great request. The animated mass of human beings and animals were a sight to be remembered, in fact, it was the sight of the day, we are sorry to say. We have omitted to notice the vast number of pedestrians of both sexes who under a boiling sun wended their way with a determination worthy of a good cause. We understand several accidents occurred, in one case in [on] the journey a gentleman had his arm broken, and we heard of a lady having an ancle [sic] broken. We wonder more casualties did not take place. The Volunteers arrived early in distant parts of the Park which had been appointed, and far from the gaze of the visitors early assembled. It was not known that the review ground had been changed from the front of the House to Cawton [Calton?]Pastures, and what is lucidly described by the Sheffield daily contempories was observed by only a few. The movements were, no doubt gone through satisfactory[sic], but it is useless filling our columns with that which was not witnessed but ought to have been. We hardly think that anyone will care to read what they particularly went to see. The only thing that could be a reward for the labour and expence [sic] was the beautiful scenery and grounds around Chatsworth with the fountains playing.

There then followed a report of the speeches and list of the various Officers and men of the different Battalions, and concludes;

We hear that it was only the previous evening that Colonel Manners determined on the alteration [*of the review ground*]. It is a pity that the public could not have had timely information, however, there was a serious hitch in the business, which as before said we hope will not act detrimentally, for all must be aware that the efficiency of the Volunteers cannot be achieved without considerable expense to its members, therefore, any breach of faith in connection with them and their friends we are sure cannot but reduce the desire to foster the movement.

The road home presented an even more animated scene as those who were willing to walk and release the horses in the morning, contemptuously refused to plod it any longer, the lower extremities having begun to fail them, some from the influence of the various quantities of liquor imbibed. We wondered how the great mass of people who inundated the pretty village of Baslow, were to be conveyed to their respective homes, The line of the route to the old town of Chesterfield was lined at every road, and the difference in the attire was marked. The muslin had undergone a large amount of pressure, and therefore, had considerably collapsed, the male costume had not been improved, all seemed jaded, and the miracle is how old hacks will have managed to land their living cargoes safe at their destination.

Thursday 8th.	Fencing where the parties had broke the fences down that came by the special trains. Then I fetched some wood from the top of the Park for Mr Drabble. Father cuting thistles a very hot day.
Friday 9th.	Leading wood for Mr Drabble from the top of the Park, sent the other half notes to Messrs. Thorpe for 20£, wrote a letter to Mr Walton about the wool, another very hot day.
Saturday 10th.	Leading wood for Mr Drabble, Father cuting thistles, rather more air today but very hot at times.
Sunday 11th.	Another very hot day, Father and George went to Ashford Feast
Monday 12th.	Jobing about in the morning then I went to Bakewell then to Ashford Feast, stope all night another hot day.
Tuesday 13th.	Got home about noon then I and Father and an Irishman called Dominick came he went with us and set some rails that was fallen down between the Farmstead and the Cowley Lydget, a very hot day.
Wedensday 14th.	Leading wood for Mr Drabble, Dominick flat howing the potatose. Father opening the soughf that brings water in the cowley lydget, a very hot day brought flour from Rowsley Station.
Thursday 15th.	Leading wood in the forenoon for Mr Drabble, I took the old cart to Pilsley in the afternoon and Mrs Turner 1 sack of flour. Sir J Paxton was intered at Edensor this day. Domn flat howing tho potatoeo, Fathor opening tho soughf for the water to run in the cowley lydget, a very hot day.
Friday 16th.	Whe began mowing the seeds in the South Field mowed rather more than half of them, Wm. Downs and James Twelves helped me, Dominick finished flat hoeiing the

potatose, Father teded part of what whe mowed, took the calves into the Farmstead, very hot dry weather.

Saturday 17th

I went to Boythorpe for 22 cwt. of coal took 2 horses I went into Chesterfield saw Mr Hardwick about the wool got home about 4 o'clock the coal is for ourselves. Beeley Club Feast today, Father and Dominic teding the seeds Wm. Downs helped them in the morning a little, a hot day.

Sunday 18th.

I went to Ashover with A Lees to see Mr and Mrs Lees, got home about 10 o'clock another hot day.

I went to Ashover with A Lees to see Mr and Mrs Lees

© Derbyshire County Council

Monday 19th.	Turned the seeds, I went to Hart Hill Hall to Mr Porters to look at his wool but whe did not bargain I offered him 60s per tod. Dominic earthed 3 rows of potatose in the afternoon a very hot day.
Tuesday 20th.	Leading the seeds lead 6 waggon loads Edward Mortin helping us and Elizabeth Grindey helping us in the afternoon. Richard Stone began with us this morning at 10s per week, a very hot day.
Wedensday 21st.	I and Richard mowing Wm. Downs and J Evans helped us a little at night whe finished mowing the South field. Domny and Father helping, Father fetched the sheep and calves out of the little brook and put them in the thorne lee and little Lydget, he took the ewes and lambs out of the mortin greave put them in the cowley lydget he took them out of the church yard to the others, rather more air today much pleasanter.
Thursday 22nd.	Richard finished teding the seeds in the forenoon dommey jobing about, Father at the Lydget I was brewing we did 3 strike half of it for G Bond. Richard and domney earthing potatose in the afternoon, a very hot day.
Friday 23rd.	Richard and I went to the station for the last of the beding that I bought of Mrs George paid her for it 14s. Father and Domney turning some of the seeds, I took the waggon and whe brought one load before dinner, Sarah Stone and Ann Grindey and our Sarah helping us in the afternoon whe got 3 loads in all today, looks like rain not quite as hot. Robert Evans helped us to get the remainder up at night. [*that is into haycocks*]
Saturday 24th.	Jobing about in the morning then broke the hay open. Richard took the horses to the smithy whe got 2 more loads in the afternoon finished getting all the hay out of that field, 11 waggon loads in all. Took the horses in the cowley lydget at night, Mr Thompson came and looked at the lambs, he is to take 4 wedensday after next not so hot today.
Sunday 25th.	The little heifer went across the river in the night to W Lees bull and was bulled, turned the milk cows in the meek field. Mr and Mrs W Lees slept here last night.
Monday 26th.	I went to Calton Lees and Calton Houses Geo Ellyth wool I bought at 56s per tod, saw Mr Hardwick he is to have the wool he is to come on Friday next. Richard opening the sough to bring water in the farmstead Domney riding up the wall sides in the bering gate that thay have rebuilt, another hot day. I rode with Mr Lees from Bakewell.
Tuesday 27th.	I and Father Richard and Thomas Gannion and Domney

all opening for the water to come in the Farmstead whe got it in the haughf? An uncommon hot day.

Wedensday 28th. Richard and Domney mowing in the mains I was brewing, then I went to Edensor saw Mr Cottingham about different matters. Took 3 year old calves into Mr Cavendish field at Calton Lees at 1s6d per week. Went to Bumper Castle and bought Mr Wilsons wool at 5s6d per tod a very hot day.

Thursday 29th. Mowing part of the day, Sarah and tommy and I and Father teding and getting some hay in the mains it rained a little but very slight. Killed ½ dozen pigeons for Mr Oldham. Mr Mayhew called made the haybarn ready for some more hay, a good deal colder

Friday 30th. Fetched 2 loads of gravel for Mr Sculthorpe, rowed some hay and cocked it up, a little rain fell in the morning. Mr Hardwick came at night and whe weighed up some wool our own allso at 58s per tod.

Saturday 1st July. Mowed till noon then whe got 2 loads of hay in the afternoon out of the mains a fine day.

Sunday 2nd. A very hot day I and the Mrs went to Edensor at night.

Monday 3rd. Ben Halksworth helping us to mow in the mains whe got 2 more loads of hay allso, a very hot day, found one lamb that had the weaks? Cliped the wool off and put oil and soot on.

Tuesday 4th. Wm. Downs helped us to mow a little in the morning whe finished the bottom end of the mains and mowed a little of the top end, I was not very well in the middle of the day, got 2 more loads of hay out of the mains, a hot day a slight shower of rain at night.

Wedensday 5th. Wm. Downs helped us to mow all day J Evans helped us a bit at night, whe finished mowing the mains got 2 more loads of hay from the bottom end 8 little waggon loads of 9 acres a poor crop, a fine day.

Thursday 6th. Some rain at intervals thunder and lightning, the men cuting thistles, teded some in the morning I went to Baslow in the afternoon went to Mr Mayhew with their sheep bought a new collar from Mr Marples bought the meal off 7qrs. oats there were left at the mill that I brought of John White.

Friday 7th. Ploughed the remainder of the bering gate and sowed the rape. Richard and Domney with me, tom mowing thistles. Went to Bakewell at night intending to see Mr Hardwick but did not see him, very heavy rain last night showers today.

Saturday 8th.

I went to Sheffield with Smedley bought a sack of peas at 5d per peck sold some at 8d. the men diging nettles in the orchard and in the hay a little. Mr Furniss called to see the chees I am to see him on Monday he bought the Lees at 68s. per cwt. .

Sunday 9th.

Beeley Feast D Milnes and Mrs and Aunt Betty came, some showers.

Monday 10th.

I went to Bakewell Market and sold the chees to Mr Furniss at 69s. per cwt. to go on Friday or Saturday. Mr Thompson sent for 4 lambs he paid me 28s each for them, Mr Hardwick did not come I want between 70 and 80£ of him. Whe went turning and got some hay up in the mains, Richard and tom mowed the Churchyard. Mother and Samuel and Sarah Pearson came allso John Elliott, Paid my Mother one years interest for 40£ due in May, ordered 9 bags of fine flour of Mr Else some slight showers.

Tuesday 11th.

Thomas and Richard and Dominick lead 7 loads of manure into the Mains, went in the hay after dinner. Mrs and I and Mrs Buckley went with us to Bakewell towards night bought one suit of clothes of W Lees and some other cloth for the children, a fine day but very gloomy.

Wedensday 12th.

In the hay all day got 4 waggon loads a fine day it looked like rain.

Thursday 13th.

Finished rakeing and spread the manure that was lead sawed some firewood, a showery day.

Friday 14th.

Took the chees to Longstone for Mr Furniss, 10cwt 2qrs. 14lb. Came back by Bakewell Mr Jackson and Lord G Cavendish was elected Members of Parliament I dined with them at the Rutland Arms got home about 4 o'clock, our lads lead 8 more loads of manure and spread it in the Mains, a heavy shower of rain about noon.

Saturday 15th.

Finished the hay in the Mains 2 more loads, fetched 1 load of coal for Rev Sculthorpe. Whe took one horse and 3 men helped Matthew Grindy to finish their hay, a fine day.

Sunday 16th.

Went to Holmesfield feast to Woodthorpe to sister Sarah's sister Farrell and John Turner Sister Mary and John Siddall and Wm. Bower was there I and Mary went to Church in the afternoon, a very hot day.

Monday 17th.

Richard and tom began mowing the Great Lydget Father and Domny got the hay out of the Churchyard, whe got home from Holmesfield about 8 o'clock a nice shower of rain.

Tuesday 18th.

Tom and Dick mowing Domny teding, I went to Pilsley took Frank Hawley 18 stone of flour, got bute shod a shower or two of rain.

Wedensday 19th.	tom and dick mowing in the Lydget domny teding, a very showery day, I made out some bills
Thursday 20th.	Finished mowing and teded and turned greater part of the Lydget, got it up into little quoil, a fine day.
Friday 21st.	Whe finis getting the hay Elizabeth and Sarah Halksworth and Elizabeth Grundy helped us a very fine day.
Saturday 22nd.	Domny went and helped Ben Halksworth with his hay, Richard and tom went to H Lees paid them the wages at night 16s and 1£ 1s. he had before, a very hot day. I went to Manchester and bought 5 sides of bacon for ourselves and 6 sides for D Milnes and ordered 4 mugs of lard. Had tea with Mrs I Grindey she went with me to see Mrs Wickers then Mr Martin and Mrs Grindy went with me to Victoria Station I went to Liverpool and stayed with Mr Travis.
Sunday 23rd.	Mr Wickers was at Mr Travis when I got there whe stayed with Mr Travis untill Sunday night then I returned to Manchester got supper with C Mortin then he went with me to Mr Wickers, Mr Wickers was just got home whe stayed with them till 12 o'clock, a very hot day.
Monday 24th.	I slept with Charles Mortin got breakfast I left Manchester by the 10 o'clock train, got to Thornbridge by 1o'clock, Had my dinner with Mr Mawrey called at Ashford, Father was in Bakewell when I got there, got home about 7 o'clock. Domny helped Ben Halksworth, a nice shower of rain in the afternoon.
Tuesday 25th.	Mowed and fetched one load of clover out of the South field, fetched 2 poads of flour from Rowsley Station went to Darley Mill paid Mr Else 27£ for flour, paid Mr Mortimer 5£ 2s 6d. for cake, Mr Hardwick came on Sunday night he paid 75£ 15s.for wool, an excessive hot day.
Wedensday 26th.	Whe packed the wool I took it to Rowsley Station, I took 2 sacks full of sacks of Thorpes and 22 of mine, brought the other load of flour with me and got boxer shod. Went to the Lees at night for the waggon, Mr Wilson came with me to Beeley I paid him for the wood 3£ 10s. I made the wagon ready to go with some wood tomorrow, a very hot day.
Thursday 27th	I went with one waggon load of posts and rails 35 scts for the new railway at Bradway got home about 6pm. Domny pulling weeds among the potatose.
Friday 28th.	Fetched one load of clover then I took some flour to Edensor and Pilsley the Mrs went with me to Bakewell, I took her forward to Ashford, got home about 9 o'clock, a fine day but cooler.

Beeley Brook
© W. H. Brighouse

Saturday 29th.	About home all day, domney cutting thistles father thatching at Lydget.
Sunday 30th.	A very fine day, my Mrs came home from Ashford at night.
Monday 31st.	I quite forgot what whe was doing this day.
Tuesday 1st August.	Mr Thompson came and bought 3 more lambs at 28s each, I took the weights to Bakewell and had them adjusted got home about 5pm, dominy cuting thistles a very hot sultry day.
Wedensday 2nd.	Fetched 2 loads of coals from Boythorpe for Mr Spencer, dominy mowing bracking some rain fell during the day.
Thursday 3rd.	James twelves began levelling in the old lane at Lydget, made ³/₄ of a day at 14s per week, dominy mowing

bracking a fine day.

Friday 4th. I went to Chesterfield for coal for ourselves brought 2 ton 1cwt, bute began of scouring she is very poorly. Jim made half a day cleaning the soughf out, Father and dominy walling the soughf a fine day.

Saturday 5th. Went to Shenton for the mare, fetched R Evans one load of coals, fetched some clover home Jim and Dominy cleaning the soughf out and walling some levelling some allso, a very hot day.

Sunday 6th. Some showers of rain fell during the day, Paid John Smith 13 weeks newspapers beginning on the last Saturday in July.

Monday 7th. I went by Baslow to Bakewell got a check changed for Mr Mayhew, went back by Baslow Mr Mayhew paid my coach fare, I got my dinner with Mr Kizitelly and Mr Mayhew Alfred Lees went with me got home between 12 and 1 o'clock. Richard Stone took boxer to the Lydget leading stones to cover the soughf and levelling a very fine day.

Tuesday 8th. I and Father and Jim dick and dominy leveling at the soughf, a fine day Paid Mr Jepson 8£ for malt

Wedensday 9th. Whe fetched one load of clover then whe all went to the wood close and began cuting oats, Jim Twelves Richard Stone Dominy Father and I, I left about 4 o'clock and my Mrs and I went to Mr Mayhew and to the concert [at] Baslow Feast, got home at 1.

Thursday 10th. Cuting oats most of the day, Richard and I fetched 16 sacks of flour, 14 cwt. bran 16cwt sharps from Rowsley Station. Raked a little a slight shower after dinner.

Friday 11th. Cuting corn till 10 o'clock then it rained untill 2 in the afternoon,cleaning the barn and the pigeon coat out and cleaned the hen run out, cut some sticks went again cuting corn and it rained again very heavy.

Saturday 12th. Dick went to Boythorpe for 18 cwt. of coal for Sculthorpe whe finished cuting oats in the wood close, went in the bering gate and cut 4 thraves it rained all afternoon.

Sunday 13th. A few showers of rain.

Monday 14th. Raked some in the morning then whe finished cuting oats in the bering gate a fine day, paid Mr Jepson 8£ for malt.

Tuesday 15th. Sawing wood &e, went into the far common piece and made a start cuting oats very showery day.

Wednesday 16th. Cuting oats in the common piece part of the day working in the old lane half the day, Mr Worrall came and looked over the oats to see if any game damages.

Thursday 17th. Cuting oats in the common piece till 11 o'clock then raked the ground that was cut. I went to the coal pit with Mr Mayhew and Mr Fearn and others to see if it was likely to find any coal but no likelyhood of coal a very showery day.

Friday 18th.   Cuting oats all day, Ben Halksworth came at night and helped us cut 75 thraves a very fine day, I wrote a letter to Thomas Gannon.

Reaping oats in a later mechanised age. Note the stooks in the foreground
© Mrs Ellis

Saturday 19th.   Jim and I went and finished cuting oats on the far side of the common piece Domney finished taking them up and raked some. Richard Jim and I mowed the seeds a second time in the South field 4 acres, Ben Halksworth Wm. Downs and J Evans came at night and helped us to finish it.

Sunday 20th.   A fine day one of our Gees missing, I expect someone hath stolen it.

Monday 21st.   I took some flower out then went to Bakewell Market forward to Mr Mayhew at Baslow, Jim and Richard leveling in the old lane, domney finished raking the far side of the common piece.

Tuesday 22nd.   Leading the wood close made one oat stack cleaned up the raking as whe went on, had to open some of the sheaves as whe pulled the stacks over a very fine day.

Wedensday 23rd. Jim raking in the hiring gate in the forenoon Richard fetched one load clover fetched Joseph Halksworth one load of coals I went rabbiting with W Lees and C Buckley caught 4, Father and domney covering the corn stack leading oats out of the bering gate in the afternoon put them in the barn.

Thursday 24th. Putting up the sheep neting in the Bering gate and railed some, Father fetched the sheep from the Lydget drawed 19 out of the ewes, some weather some thaves and a few of the oldest sheep and 2 tup lambs making 21, put them on the rape. Domney took 20 ewes to the little brook put the other lambs in the croft, Dick and Jim walling up some gaps after whe had finished fenceing a very wet day.

Friday 25th. Whe all went to the far common piece cuting oats, Father and Dick left us at 10 o'clock to go to the clover, Jane Halksworth and Sarah Stone and Elizabeth went with them, W Downs helped them at night thay got it up in little quoil. Jim and Domney and I cut nearly 70 thraves, a very fine day.

Saturday 26th. Sarah Stone Jane Halksworth and Ben and W Downs helped us at night to lead the South Field we had 3 wagon loads and 4 cart loads of clover out of it, made a stack of it I think about 4 tons, a very fine day. Mr Jepson called I paid him all I owed him for malt, he had one ham paid me for it 29s.

Sunday 27th. A very Hot day excessive hot.

Monday 28th. It began to rain about 7am it rained at times most of the day, Richard and Domney cleaned the harness in the forenoon, I went to the smithy and got a pin mended belonging to the thrashing machine whe thrashed some in the afternoon, Jim Twelves did not come.

Tuesday 29th. Whe finished cuting the oats, Jim Twelves came about 11am of the clock got home about 2 pm Jim and Domney leveling in the old lane the day out. Dick I and Father winnowed 2qrs. of good oats 3 strike for the horses I took them to Baslow Mill, Dick in the garden the day out. Father went to the Bering Gate to stop the sheep out of Ludlams field, a very fine day.

Wedensday 30th. Loading oats from the far common piece had 5 waggon loads Jim didn't come, made a stack on the middle brandery a very fine day.

Thursday 31st. Lead 2 more waggon loads from the far common piece and fetched one load bracking rather a showery day.

Friday 1st Sept. Finished leading corn Dick rakeing in the forenoon whe fetched one load of rakings and one load of sheaves after dinner. A fine day, got some pears in the afternoon.

Saturday 2nd.

Dick and Domny leveling in the old lane pulled the clover stack in the morning, toped it up and spun some ropes Father began thatching it, I went and looked the sheep about 11 o'clock in the rape, fetched the horse in, got my dinner took Charles Buckley to the Station. Looked the sheep again before 2 pm I found one dead, I think it was poisoned. Got some early potatose 2 thirds of them is bad then I skinned the sheep sold the skin for 3s. cut it up and boiled it for the pigs, a fine growing day.

Sunday 3rd.

I went to Baslow to Mr Mayhews with Alfred Lees got home about 10pm, had some talk with Mr Kizitelly about going abroad with him.

Monday 4th.

Domney took the sheep out of the Little Brook and took them in the fr common piece then he finished getting the early potatose Father and I went to Bakewell Market I came home with H Lees. Sent F Travis a newspaper sent him a carpet bag full of pares [pears], wrote to Thorpes for prices sent them half notes when completed for 40£, a very fine day, sent a check on Saturday to the Paraffin Light Compy. for 3£ 8s. ordered 2 more casks of oil.

Tuesday 5th.

I went to Sheffield with with Smedley sold some apples 8pks. at 1s 8d. 4 pks. pears at 1s 8d. sold wesmalens [westmorelands?] apples at 15d.Domney getting potatose Father thatching.

Wedensday 6th.

I was jobing about home in the morning sent an order for Indian corn to Mr Heighton of Nottingham, went to Miss Waltons sale did not buy anything, Father thatching a very fine day. Domney getting potatose fetched one cart load of potatose home at night.

Thursday 7th.

Fetched 2 loads of gravel for Rev Sculthorpe from the broad meadow went to look at Mr Jarrett chees for Mr Parker, wrote to him about it. Got some apples and pairs at night, Erbut Buckley helped me Father thatching, a very fine day.

Friday 8th.

Gathering apples in the forenoon 8 pks of the large ones and 24 of wesmalans. Bought 11 pks of Matth. Grindey 9 of John Turner 24 of Charles Cocker and 8 pks more of Cockers went to Bakewell in the afternoon Mrs went with me, came back by Pilsley borrowed John Oxsprings cart to take apples to Sheffield tomorrow Domney got some more potatose in the morning he went with Ben Halksworth in the afternoon in the moor for one load of bracking, a very fine day.

Saturday 9th.

I went to Sheffield with the apples, Father thatching,

Domney getting potatose he finished getting the red ones, Father and him fetched another load home a very good crop of red ones 2 good cart loads a fine day. I called at Baslow Mill as I came home and bought the meal of 2qrs of oats, Sarah Halksworth came with me from Baslow she left Gardams.

Sunday 10th. A roughf wind but a fine day.

Monday 11th. Jobing about in the forenoon I went to Pilsley in the afternoon with the cart I borrowed, got boxer shod Domney getting potatose he helped Ben Halksworth to fetch another load of bracking, Father thatching a very hot day, took the hoggs into the churchyard.

Tuesday 12th. Went to Boythorpe for two loads of coals for Mr Sculthorpe, Father thatching, Domney geting potatose. Bought 9pks of apples of Simeon Goodwin at 11d 7pks at 7d per peck 6 pks at 8d bought 14pks of Mr Cocker at 11d 7pks at 7d per peck a very sultry day.

Wednesday 13th. Went to Holmesfield with the apples and sold them all very readily. Domney getting potatose, Father thatching another very hot day, I got home between10 and 11 o'clock.

Thursday 14th. Not doing very much today, very tyred after my journey yesterday. Domney getting potatose Father thatching another very hot day.

Friday 15th. Went for coals for Mr Sculthorpe 2 ton 1 cwt, another very hot day Domney finished getting potatose, thay are going bad very fast, Father thatching, Sent one cask of paraffin oil to Ashford to Milnes.

Saturday 16th. Fetched the potatose home, went to Rowsley to see if the flour was come, got an envoice of 21 sacks of flour and 10 sacks fine sharps from Newark allso envoice of 10qrs. of Indian Corn and 2 qrs. of Millett from Messrs Sturge of Birmingham. Got one sack of Indian Meal and one sack of flour of Mr Evans of Allport.

Sunday 17th. Very hot day Saul Magson went home tonight, Edwin and Ellen Milnes came from Ashford, took the milk cows into Mr Cavendish field at Lees yesterday at 4d per week each.

Monday 18th. I and Father went to Bakewell Market, Domney and I fetched the flour from the Station delivered a good deal of flour and sharps out, another very hot day.

Tuesday 19th. I went to Boythorpe for coal for Mr Sculthorpe 2 tons, then I went to Shaws sale at Rowsley then I fetched 16pks of apples from Mr Worralls that I bought last night at 10d per pk. 7 pecks of damsons from Henry Hibberts. Father got 5 pks of our damsons, Domney jobing about, a very hot day.

Wednesday 20th.	Went to Holmesfield with the apples and damsons sold them all, got home a little before 10pm. I took Mr Mayhew 2 galls of paraffin oil and one gallon a week since, Father getting apples, Domney jobing about a little rain fell at night.
Thursday 21st.	Domney fetched the Indian Corn up yesterday, I took 4qrs of the Indian and 1qr of the Millet to the mill to be ground today, righting books and many other jobs. Domney horling? potatose Father getting some apples, I bought another goose for 6s 6d. I sold her for 7s. a very fine day.
Friday 22nd.	Fetched 2 loads of coals from Boythorpe for ourselves, Domney in the garden Father getting apples, rather cooler today but a very fine day.
Saturday 23rd.	Fetched another 2 loads of coals from Boythorpe for ourselves, Domney in the garden Father getting apples a very hot day.
Sunday 24th.	A very hot day.
Monday 25th.	I went to Manchester bought 2 sides of bacon and took the pot to be filled with lard, paid on Act. 5£ called to see Mary Ann and Isaac Grindey took them a few apples went to the Bell view [Belle Vue] gardins, got home about 1am. The fireworks were splendid. Father went to Chesterfield Fair, Domney diging nettles in the croft Benjamin Halksworth had boxer to take his chees to the fair, a very fine day very hot.
Tuesday 26th.	Jobing about, I went to the Hill Top paid Mr H Lees for his sheep that I bought of him 8£ 8s. Father and I got a few apples, Domney diging up nettles in the croft, a very hot day.
Wednesday 27th.	Fetched 2 tons of coals from Boythorpe for Mr Sculthorpe. Father jobing about got a few apples, Domney diging up nettles in the croft and burning them an excesssive hot day.
Thursday 28th.	We were sheep diping at Hill top, Diped 137 sheep rather cooler but a fine day
Friday 29th.	Went to Rowsley paid the Railway carriage on Indian corn 1£ 4s 5d from Glocester, fetched 3 loads of wood out of the plantain for Mr Buckley, Domney getting damasins Father and I got about 25 pks of apples. Robert Halksworth fetched one hive of bees to the halves? W Hutchinson brought 4 pks of Damasins at 11d per peck cooler but a fine day.
Saturday 30th.	Went to Totley with the apples and damasins sold the Matthews at 1s 6d. per pk Damsins at 1s 4d. westmalans at 1s 4d. Shephards at 1s 2d, wind fallen at 1s per pk, sold

all I had, called at Storth House, Domney and Father getting apples a fine day.

Sunday 1st October.	A very hot day.
Monday 2nd.	Went to Bakewell Market bought 8 pigs of Tom Allsop at 42s each, James Stone had one at 43s Mr Worrall 2 at 43s each Mr Marsden 1 at 43s Robt. Halksworth 1 at 44s. Domney diging up nettles a very hot day.
Tuesday 3rd.	Making bills out part of the day took some flower out Domney diging up nettles, Fetched bacon and lard from the Station. Mr Spencer paid me his bill a very hot day.
Wedensday 4th.	Bakewell Cattle Show took the gees and Butter did not get a prize, Domney getting up nettles, Dinner with the members at Mr Greaves, got home about 10 o'clock a very fine day.
Thursday 5th.	Not doing much Mr Thompson fetched 3 fat sheep at 8½d per lb. Earthed up the Salary [celery], wrote 4 letters sent half notes to Thorpes for 20£.Father got the remainder of the damasins, Domney getting up nettles a very fine day excessively hot.
Friday 6th.	Fetched 2 loads of coals for Ben Halksworth from Boythorpe got home about 1 o'clock. Mr Lees sold us one pig to Mr Ward at 8s per stone to go on the 17th. David Milnes and his Sister in Law came from Ashford, Sampson Hodgkinson came from Father, sold him some oak sawing 10 feet at 1s per foot 8 feet at 8d. per foot a very hot day.
Saturday 7th.	To[ok] Sampson Hodgkinson the oak 2 pieces 9 feet long each and 7¼ inches broad. Brought Mr Spencer 2 tons of coal from Stubley paid for it 12s, expenses and toll bars 4s, Father jobing about home, Domney diging up nettles very foggy in the morning, a fine day. In the margin: brought milk cows from the Lees.
Sunday 8th.	Some rain a few showers.
Monday 9th.	Boxer helped Mrs Holmes in the Gardens with a furniture van for Lady Paxton, Father sorting potatose. Some men called from Sheffield I sold them 27pecks of apples at 1s3d. per pk 1£ 13s 9d, sent the remaining half notes to Newark, walled up a gap at the top of the croft, a good deal of rain fell, some very heavy showers.
Tuesday 10th.	Killed one pig for ourselves then I and Domney, Henry and George fetched the stirks and the black horse off Calton, paid the adjoicement [agistment?] at Edensor 7£ 15s then I went to Wm. Lees and killed 2 pigs, wrote a letter to the Paraffin Light Compy. at Birmingham with one half 5£ note, took the stirks in the farmstead and the black horse in the Pits, some very heavy rain during the night

'Killed one pig for ourselves'
© S. J. Saklatvala

Wedensday 11th.	Cut up the pig 19 stones 19lbs, sold most of the sparerib. Went to Bakewell Mr Wells paid me for one goose I sent him last week sold Mr Orme one for next week. Wm Lees and I went rabbiting caught 8 full grown and 5 young ones fetched the stirks out of Mr Cavendish field a showery day
Thursday 12th.	Cleaning out the cowhouse and began whitewashing sent the last half 5£ note to the Paraffin Compy. Sent 22£ to Messrs, Thorpe of Newark when completed, sold George Wilson 10 sheep at 45s each, a showery day.
Friday 13th.	Went to [H]Athersage Fair took Mr Mayhew a goose sent one to Mr Wells each weighing 8¼ lbs. when dressed, domney and Father witewashing the cow house and Fotherham, a showery day. [*Fotherham — fodder room*]
Saturday 14th.	Domney fiished witewashing the cow house began the calf place. I went to Burchover and bought one shearling ram of Mr Heathcoat gave 3£ 3s. for him, got bute shod of one foot, it turned out a fine day.
Sunday 15th.	A fine day,
Monday 16th.	Killed one pig to take to Chesterfield tomorrow for Mr Ward then Father and I went to Bakewell Fair. Sold Mr Parker one chees to go Thursday, Paid Mr Evans 2£ 11s for 1 sack of flour and 1 sack of Indian Meal. Paid Mr

'Went to Hathersage Fair'
© Derbyshire County Council

Cavendish's man 8£ 17s 6d for adjoicement of stirks and milk cows, Domney witewashing, some slight showers.

Tuesday 17th.
Took the pig to Mr Ward of Chesterfield it rained Havens hard all the way, I went and brought 2 loads of coals back I got a very bad cold, Domney witewashing took G Holmes 1 load of coals, a fine afternoon.

Wedensday 18th.
Fetched 2 sacks of flour and 120 stones of fourths from the station, fetched Joseph Halksworth 1 ton of coals then I took flour to Edensor and Pilsley got Boxer removed all round [*All his shoes removed*] fetched meal of 3qrs of oats from Baslow Mill I bought the oats of H Lees 86 pecks of meal, weighed the chees 12 cwt. 0qrs. 12lbs. 77 cheeses. Domney finished witewashing the stable and Father jobing about home, a fine day.

Thursday 19th.
Took the chees it weighed 1lb less at Chesterfield, brought 2 loads of coal for ourselves Domney finished witewashing the stable, he went in the top of the Mains in the afternoon leveling, a fine day but cold.

Friday 20th.
Got the coals, in, righting books, Fetched Miss Hawkins 2 loads of coals, took Mr Deeley 5 cwt. of bran he paid me for it. Took John Thompson 1 sack of flour, Domney leveling in the Mains a fine day.

Saturday 21st.
Pited [*stored*] 25 pecks of apples, fetched the sheep home belted the 20 ewes and marked them & 12 hoggs took 2

hoggs and 2 cows in Henry Hilberts field the cows 3s 6d per week, took 2 hoggs and 2 cows in George Banks field on Thursday. Paid John Smith 2s 2d the second quarter ending last Saturday in January 1866 for the Sheffield and Rotherham newspaper. The cows crossed the river into H Lees meadow a very fine day Domney finished leveling the dirt in the top of the Mains.

Sunday 22nd.	A fine day.
Monday 23rd.	Went to the Lydget in the morning then I wrote 4 letters took the sheep netting up in the Bering gate, Domney and Father piting potatose a fine day.
Tuesday 24th.	Sold Charles Fearn 2 sheep at 52s each, brought them home and the ram allso turned the ram to the ewes one tuped. Father went to Matlock Fair it rained hard this morning, Domney leveling and nocking sods in the croft.
Wedensday 25th.	Put the remainder of the apples by to keep then I went to Mr Sybery's sale at Snitterton Hall things sold very dear. Domney began witewashing the new cow house, Father jobing about it rained in the morning allso very cold day.
Thursday 26th.	Went to Bakewell then killed John Elliott one pig. Bought 2 pigs of Mr Thompson for 10£ 5s, Domney witewashing it rained very heavy most of the day.
Friday 27th.	Fetched the Indian meal of 3qrs. of corn then I took 2qrs of oats from W Lees to Baslow one qr. for meal and the other for Mr Mayhew. Domney witewashing, I put Mrs Mayhew's spitefull in the light cart, a fine day.
Saturday 28th.	Jobing about took Mr Thompson 1 sack Ind. Meal then I and Father and Domney brought the rails out of the Bering gate, sent 18£ 8s to Messrs. Sturge of Birmingham. Put the rails up at the top of the cow house straightened up the turnip house and several other jobs, a very fine day.
Sunday 29th.	It rained very hard most of the day.
Monday 30th.	I went to [New] Haven Fair Father went to Bakewell Market Domney took Bute to Rowsley to have her shod he was there most of the day, a very fine day. Mr Sculthorpe called and paid his bill at night.
Tuesday 31st.	Ground 2 strike of malt and brewed for ourselves. Shenton called and whe seatoned the calves, Domney diging up nettles in the orchard. Hadfield called and tried to buy 1 pig he bid 10£ 10s, I ofered it for 10£ 16s, Jobing about the remainder of the day, a fine day.
Wedensday 1st Nov.	I and Domney fetched 2 loads of wood for the Rev. Sculthorpe from opposite Harewood fetched 2 loads of sand in the afternoon and several other jobs, took the black

horse in the cow close, a very fine day.

Thursday 2nd. Killed one pig the sanded on, Killed 4 gees one for Shenton and one for Mr Mayhew one for Wm. Downs and one for Mr Wells. Jobing about the remainder of the day, a fine day slight rain at night.

Friday 3rd. Cut up the pig and sold a good deal of the pork the pig weighed 25 stones, then I took Mr Mayhew their goose I called at Chatsworth as I came home again, saw Mr Cottingham he promised to come to Beeley either Monday or Wedensday. A fine day, Domney nocking manure in the Mortin greave and pits.

Saturday 4th. I went to S Mawreys sale at Thornbridge he had a very good sale, Domney witewashed the hen roost, a very fine day.

Sunday 5th. Peter Milnes came from Ashford, he paid me for 5 pecks of malt and 1½ lbs of hops that thay had a year since, a very fine day.

Monday 6th. Lead 8 loads of stone from the Ldget into the yard to pitch it, Domney with me, 14 sheep tupt. The duke's party was shooting partridges about Beeley thay shot about 30 brace, a fine day.

Tuesday 7th. Lead 9 loads of manure in the mains then I went looking the cattle and sheep and went to Graftons bought Saml. Gardners pig 3£ 15s. Sold John Oxspring one 4£ 5s. a fine day rain at night.

Wedensday 8th. Domney witewashing the granary, I was writing in the morning took the stirks in Mr Marsdens field, a rainy day.

Thursday 9th. Fetched 4 loads of stone from the Lydget, Domney finished witewashing the granary a fine day, took 2 qrs. of Ind corn to the mill.

Friday 10th. Mending sacks all day, Domney thrashing a few oats a fine day.

Saturday 11th. Mending sacks in the morning, sent them off to Newark in the afternoon, 30 of mine 36 of Thorpes, Domney riding? in the far common piece a fine day, the keeper sent us a hare.

Sunday 12th. A very fine day Aunt and Elizabeth came from Ashord.

Monday 13th. I and Father went to Bakewell Domney riding in the common piece Mr H Lees paid me for the pig I sold him and the sheep.G Wilson broke the axle of his cart coming home from Bakewell, a fine day.

Tuesday 14th. Sent 50£ 18s to Thorpes of Newark, Mr Worral paid me the game damages 15£ 9s. I killed Mr Lees his pig Domney riding in the common piece a fine day. I burned some thorns in the wood close.

Wedensday 15th.	Cut Mr Lees pig up in the morning, went in the far common piece to Domney and Father whe were riding untill noon thay were riding all day. I went to Edensor and paid the rent then I went to Baslow to Mr Mayhew, went back to Baslow and dined with Mr Cottingham, got home about 10 o'clock a very fine day.
Thursday 16th.	I went to Edensor in the morning then I took bute to Rowsley had a shoe set on, Domney and Father riding all day a very fine day.
Friday 17th.	Wm. Downs came whe began pitching the yard one horse leading the dirt away, Domney and Father and I all working in the yard a fine day.
Saturday 18th.	Wm. Downs, I and Father and Domney, at the pitching one horse leading the dirt, a very fine day.
Sunday 19th.	A very dirty wet day.
Monday 20th.	Wm. Downs I and father and Domney, at the pitching one horse leading dirt and stone for pitching, a shower or two of rain.
Tuesday 21st.	Wm. Downs and Father pitching, Richard Stone and Domney leading dirt and stone with 2 horses. I went to Sheffield with Smedley. Put 31£ belonging to my Mother into the Sheffield and Rotherham Bank in my name and my sister Sarah's name jointly to be divided equally amongst my sisters and myself at my Mothers death, a fine day but very roughf wind
Wedensday 22nd.	Richard Stone and Domney leading stone and dirt in the forenoon with 2 horses, thay lead 4 loads of manure on the mains in the afternoon, thay did some choping. Wm. Downs I and Father pitching untill noon then it rained so hard it was not fit to stand out for some time. Whe killed a big pig in the afternoon, a very roughf day.
Thursday 23rd.	Domney leading stone and dirt with one horse. Wm. Downs I and Father pitching. Mr Leech came to inspect our cattle and premises whe have insured them in the Bakewell Insurance Society. Cut the pig up at night it weighed 30 stones [*210kgs*]. A very deal of rain fell last night and very roughf wind. I engaged Wm. White for 16£ a year to come on Monday or Tuesday next..
Friday 24th.	2 horses leading stone and dirt, Wm. Downs Jacob Towndrow and Father pitching the yard. Received an envoice from Newark for 52£ 15s 6d. a very fine day.
Saturday 25th.	Wm. Downs pitching some of the day, a miserable wet day, Domney choping some and jobing about. I fetched 2 loads of flour and offals from the Station, Mr Thompson and Mr Tomlinson had ¹/₂ ton of bran. Wm. Downs and I fixed the

stove in the Kitchen chamber.

Sunday 26th.   A very dirty windy day.

Monday 27th.   I fetched the remainder of the flour and offals from the station, then I helped Wm. Downs and Jacob Towndrow to pitch in the yard, a fine day, Domney jobing about Father helping us to pitch.

Tuesday 28th.   Jacob Towndrow and I finished pitching the yard. Wm. White came he and Domney leading dirt out of the yard in the morning, thay took 3 loads of manure in the afternoon in the mains, he fetched 1 load of coals for Joseph Halksworth, rather a dirty day.

Wedensday 29th.   I went to Pilsley in the morning and got a chain mended left the plough to have a new share and new slipes, got a piece of iron put on the light cart shaft. Wm. White and Domney spreading manure in the mains, Domney went to Bakewell and got measured for some new clothes. I paid Mr Jepson for 2 qrs of malt 5£ 15s. all I owe him, a fine day.

Thursday 30th.   I went with Wm. to Woodhouse for 2 tons of hard coal for Mr Spencer, Domney nocking manure in the mains, rather a dirty day.

December 1865 – May 1866

December starts with news of an outbreak of cattle plague, not as we might have supposed, Foot and Mouth, but Rinderpest, a virulent disease of cattle. Bakewell Market is closed and movement of cattle restricted, it all has a familiar ring! There is no compensation for the unfortunate farmer, and the Duke's offer of assistance was no doubt very welcome.

The remainder of the diary is very much taken up with the day-to-day matters on the farm. I wonder how much input his wife had in the enlargement of the garden and the paving of the Courtyard, much of which is still to be seen today?

I regret not knowing the conclusion of his discussions with Mr Jepson, the Licensee from Edensor, about taking over the running of the Post Buses and stables.

It seems remarkable to us today, the distances that had to be walked. For example, on May 5th , William sent his two sons, Henry and George at that time 8 and 6, to walk from Beeley to his brother George's farm at Storth House, a distance of 10 or 12 miles, with a message.

William did eventually move to Bridge Farm and take over running the corn mill nearby in the Park. His grandson Albert, farmed at Norman House, the last of the Hodkins to do so, until he retired in 1960.

Friday 1st December. Wm. ploughing in the wood close, Domney riding in the far common piece, I was jobing about in the forenoon, I went to Bakewell in the afternoon brought 1 gall of gin from Mr Ormes I did not pay for it. Wm. leading dirt in the wood close with boxer in the afternoon. I bought Wm. Whites chees at 63s per cwt. for Mr Coates of Owler Bar, sent him one chees 23lb. The remainder I must send him Friday next week by John Smith, a very fine day.

Saturday 2nd. Wm. ploughing Domney spreading the dirt that Wm. led yesterday, then he was spreading dropings in the cow close, I was jobing about and writing in the morning.

Sunday 3rd. A fine day.

Monday 4th. Wm. ploughing in the wood close, a fine day.

Tuesday 5th. Stubing an apple in the top of the orchard began clearing rubbish away for to make the garden, a very fine day, Wm. ploughing.

Note: To Stub, to remove a tree stump.

Wedensday 6th. Thrashing and winnowing 4 qrs. of oats took them to Mr Mortimers Mill for meal, 1 sack to be split for the horses, rained in the morning but a fine day after. Mr Cottigham came at night and looked round.

Thursday 7th. Wm. ploughing, Domney Father and I making the garden ready, I pruned the cherry tree.

Friday 8th. Thrashing part of the day winnowed the rakeings, finished thrashing all there was in the barn. Caught many mice, Domney went to see for a place at Longstone, a fine day.

Saturday 9th. Pulling down the old wall in the garden, Wm. ploughing in the morning, fetched the meal from the mill in the afternoon, then he pulled up some rails in the garden. I was pruning the apple tree in the garden got an apple pit in.sent an order for for 1 ton of cake for ourselves and 1 ton for Mr Thompson, a very fine day.

Sunday 10th. I went to Ashford Henry went with me, I had intended going on to Dove Holes to see Uncle Charles but was too late for the train, a very fine day.

Monday 11th. Took Mr Deeley 5cwt of bran got bute shod of one foot, took her to Wm. he was ploughing, he finished the wood close. I went to Bakewell market, sale of cattle prohibited for 3 months on account of the cattle plague, a very fine day.

Tuesday 12th. Bought 1 cwt 3 qrs 10lbs.of chees for Mr Coates of Owler Bar took him 2 pecks of apples for Mr Slater 2 pks for Josh Biggin 2 for Mother 2 for sister Sarah. Wm brought 2 ton 2 cwt. of coal for ourselves from Woodhouse. I rode with the coach from Owler Bar to Baslow called at Mr

Mayhews, Kisitelly was very drunk I helped to put him to bed, Domney nocking dung a very fine day.

Wedensday 13th.

Wm. fetched the new cart from Pilsley, got the coals in took Wm. Downs some, manuring the garden, took Mr Tomlinson 1 sack of flour Mrs Cooper 2 hams Mrs Buxton $1/2$ bag of flour. Domney nocking manure in the morning, whe winnowed some oats in the afternoon, rather frosty but a fine day.

Thursday 14th.

Ridled some chaff, took R Evans 3 sacks Wm. White one sack. Killed 1 pig 15 stones, fetched the cake up and the Indian corn took 5 qrs. to the mill 5qrs. home. Domney nocking dung, Mr Worral called and set the garden wall out he promised to send 2 men in a few days, afine day but rather frosty.

Friday 15th.

Wm, and Domney cuting a soughf up the side of the wood close, I took some tiles on, cut up the pig sent Mr Jackson half notes 15£ for cake, a very fine day.

Saturday 16th.

Wm. and Domney soughing I helped them most of the day, filled it up with small stones. Sent 40£ to Thorpes of Newark, a very fine day James Wilson sent us 43lbs of beef at $5^1/2$d lb.

Sunday 17th.

Fine day.

Monday 18th.

Wm. and Domney leveling a bank off up the side of wood close, dikeing on bottom of bull balk, put 2 sheep in George Bonds field, Borrowed 3£ 10s. of Mr Buckley. Killed George Holmes pig, rather a dull day. Sent Mr Jackson the remaining half notes and check 18£ for cake.

Tuesday 19th.

Wm. leading manure, lead 10 loads into the mains, whe took a troughf to set in the bottom of the great lydget between H Lees and us. It used to stand on the other side of the road just below our house. Domney dikeing bottom of bull balk and top end of cow close. Father went to to Potters sale of Winsley. I was writing all forenoon, one letter to Thorpes one to J Grindey one to Mr Travis one to Mr Outram one to Mrs Bryan and one newspaper to Mr Travis, a very dull day rain at night, cut G Holmes pig 20 stones 6lb. I went to Wm.Downs wedding at night.

Wedensday 20th.

Wm. and Domney spreading manure and nocking in the mains. I went to Vickers sale at Calton Lees bought 3 lots of turnips 2£ 1s. Wm. brought 2 carts for two loads at night, a very fine day.

Thursday 21st.

George Bond and Matth. Downs began acting pales on the bottom end of the new garden whe are making, Wm. Domney and I helping them part of the day. Wm. and Domney fetched the remainder of the turnips from lees, a very fine day.

Friday 22nd.	Helping G Bond and M Downs to set the pales all day, Wm. helping allso a very fine day, John Turner and Wm. Edge pulling the wall down next to Grindey in the afternoon, a very fine day.
Saturday 23rd.	Helping M Downs and G Bond seting pales Wm. and Domney helping allso and clearing away rubbish a very fine day.
Sunday 24th.	A fine day.
Monday 25th.	Christmas Day. A fine day.
Tuesday 26th.	Wm. helping G Bond and M Downs seting pales Domney left us this morning, he went to live with Mr Shaw of Rowsley, I went to Ashford to stay all night at D Milnes, a fine day.

'I went to Ashford to stay all night at D Milnes'
© Derbyshire County Council

Wedensday 27th.	Got home at 9am went with my Mrs to Rowsley Station at 1 pm she went to her cousin at Longstone. I was looking at them coursing in the afternoon. Wm. helping G Bond and Matth. Downs seting pales, fine day. I went to Longstone allso by the 7.20 train at night.
Thursday 28th.	Mrs and I got home again by the 9am train, Wm. began ploughing in the south field, I went with him and helped him to start. Killed Buckley a pig helped G Bond and M Downs a little, the church singers came at night, a fine day.
Friday 29th.	Wm. ploughing in the morning some rain about noon. Whe

fetched some flour up in the afternoon, D Milnes and S Mawry came at noon, whe had W Lees and H and Mrs Lees, Jane Buckley to tea and supper. Cut Buckleys pig up. John Downs and Wm. Downs began walling next to Grindey yesterday and today.

Saturday 30th.

Wm. ploughing part of the day G Bond and M Downs walling down side of the garden, John and Wm Downs walling next to Grindey. Whe had a pigeon shooting in the afternoon Thomas Ashton, J Reding and T Wilson shot, I and Greation and W Lees my party lost whe had a first rate supper at Mrs Holmes after, a fine day.

Sunday 31st.

Missed a day.

Monday January.

1st 1866. Got a stack of oats in then I went to Bakewell to a meeting of the Cattle Insurance. John and Wm. Downs walling, Matthew Downs and George Bond cuting a soughf and making some pales ready, a very fine day.

Tuesday 2nd.

Wm. took some flour to Edensor he went to Birchill Brickyard brought 100 9 inch tiles, he took 3 sacks of oats to Edensor Mill. John and Wm. Downs siting the Ashler by the side of the court, George Bond and Matth Downs cuting the soughf and putting tiles in. John thrashed some in the afternoon, G Bond and Matth. Downs helped us, a miserable wet day.

Wedensday 3rd.

Wm. ploughing Geo. Bond and Matth. Downs putting up the pales at the end of the kitchen, cuting out the soughf from Ludlams slopstone. I went coursing in the afternoon, a Sheffield party was here, went to Edensor at night had some talk with Mr Jepson about taking the posting of him allso the yard and taproom. John Downs finished putting up the ashlar wall then he went to Ludlams. A very fine day.

Thursday 4th.

Wm. ploughing G Bond and Matth. Downs finished putting up the pales at the end of the kitchen, Jobing about most of the day writing a little a showy [showery?] day.

Friday 5th.

Wm. went to the brickyard for 600 red bricks to line a tank with, he went ploughing in the afternoon. I helped Matth. Downs and George Bond to lay the paving down by the end of the kitchen, a fine day.

Saturday 6th.

Wm. lead space loads of manure in the mains then he helped me weel some dirt out of the garden, he took 3 loads away. I was moveing clay and soil most of the day. G Bond and Matth. Downs finished cuting the soughf then thay began cuting out the tank to hold the waste from our house and kitchen and Ludlams house, a very frosty day.

Sunday 7th.	Rather a stormy day roughf wind I went to Baslow to see Mr Mayhew at night.
Monday 8th.	Wm. fetched two loads of coals from Rowsley one for J Halkworth one for Mr Sculthorpe. Then he went to the brickyard for 400 bricks, 140 5inch and 60 4 inch pipes.Whe thrashed about an hour after he got home, G Bond and Matth. Downs was working on the tank all day when it was fit, a very showery day very roughf wind.
Tuesday 9th.	Wm. ploughing, G Bond and Matth. Downs soughfing, got the pipes and bricks in, I was helping them a fine day.
Wedensday 10th.	Wm. helping G Bond and Matth. Downs in the orchard makeing the tank and soughf. I made some edging stones. My Mrs went to Ashford I took her in the light cart, a frosty day.
Thursday 11th.	I and Wm. seting edging stones and making a border, Matth. George and Charles Fearn soughfing &e., a frosty day.
Friday 12th.	Wm. coal leading to Chatsworth, my Mrs came home from Ashford, I was looking after the cattle and helping Wm. got bute shod in the morning, he got boxer shod at night. Sent Messrs. Thorpe half notes 40£, a fine frosty day.
Saturday 13th.	Thrashing part of the day, whe finished thrashing all there was in the barn, Geo. Buckley and Erbut helping us. Father very lame of Rumatism in one knee, he cannot walk. A good deal of snow fell this morning,Wm took two loads of coal to Chatsworth, it began thawing the snow wastes very fast.
Sunday 14th.	A fine day, the snow is all gone.
Monday 15th.	Wm. leading coal to Chatsworth, I sold the black nose cow to Thos. Cocker 14£. Geo. Bond and Matth. Downs finished walling and soughfing. A fine day Father very lame yet.
Tuesday 16th.	Put the ewes in the mains, put 8 hoggs and 2 ewes in the mortin greave, fetched the 2 cows out of G Bonds field. Father very lame, Mr Else brought me 9 bags fine flour, 2 bags of bean flour and one side of bacon. I was looking after the cattle. Sent Messrs. Thorpe the remaining half notes 40£. I went down to Mr Else last night and settled with hom up to this date. I killed Mr Marsden one little pig cut it up at night. It rained very hard in the morning, Wm. leading coal to Chatsworth.
Wednesday 17th.	Looking up sacks sent two bundles 52 in number to Messrs. Thorpe, sent one paraffin cask to Birmingham, Wm. leading coal, called at Mr Graftons he paid me all he owes me. Whe brewed 3 bushells malt made 37 gallons, a very roughf wind some rain, I was looking after the cattle,

Father rather better.

Thursday 18th. Wm. leading coal, I was looking after the cattle, went to Bakewell for Shenton to one of the cows she had got a bad crush on one of her thighs, a fine day, father rather better. Paid Mr Shenton for last year ending 31st. December 1865.

Friday 19th. Wm. took 2 loads of coals to Chatsworth then he fetched Miss Hawkins one load then whe got a stack in. Dick Stone and I helping, whe was shaking straw and cleaning up the oats, winnowed some allso in the morning. Father looking after the cattle, a very roughf wind. Shenton sent some ?? and 6 powders for the horses.

Saturday 20th. Winnowing 4 qrs. oats Dick Stone and I, Wm. ploughing in the forenoon, Dick dug the soughf where the rabbitts have made holes, made them up, working in the garden about 1 hour. Whe thrashed about 1 hour after dinner then Wm. fetched 4 bags Indian Meal from the mill, the produce from 2 qrs. of Indian corn, allso the meal of 2 qrs. of oats, then Dick and Wm. went to the Burnt wood for 2 loads paving. Peter Mlnes came at night, recvd. 3 letters one from Mr Travis 2 from the Paraffin light Company, a very fine day.

Sunday 21st. Rather a showery day, Peter Milnes stoped with us all day and all night again.

Monday 22nd. Wm. ploughing in the South Field, I was working in the garden after dinner, I went to Edensor at night saw Mr Jepson had some talk with him about takeing to his buss horses and all his carriages and the yard and tap room. Called at Mr Halls and Mr Spencers, a fine day.

Tuesday 23rd. Wm. went for coals for Mr Spencer he brought 2 tons 2 cwt. I was working in the garden all day. John Downs, Wm. Downs, Isaac Grindey & Charles Fearn working in the court yard all day. Cawdwell called to look at the fat cow yesterday he bid 18£ 10s for her, I wanted 20£ for her. Father looking after the cattle, a very fine day.

Wedensday 24th. Wm. ploughing I went with Geo Wilson to Mr Fretwells sale, bought a dock grub and heavy hoe 1s 6d. paid James Wilson for 43 lbs. beef 19s 9d. Whe heard that Mrs Drabble of Harwood hath got the rinderpest. Father looking after the cattle, a very fine day but rather cold. John Downs, Wm. Downs, Isaac Grindey and Frank Staveley working at our place, Frank hanging the garden gate

Thursday 25th. Wm. ploughing, I got the black horse shod in the morning, working in the garden in the afternoon, Father looking after the cattle. Mrs Drabble hath lost 5 cows of the rinderpest. John Downs, Wm. Downs and Isaac Grindey finished repairing the flaging in the Court, Frank Staley hung the orchard gate, a very fine day.

Friday 26th.

Wm. finished ploughing the south field in the forenoon, whe thrashed some after dinner. Wm fetched one load of coals for Robert Evans, I was working in the garden in the forenoon, I took the black horse to George Anthony and stoped there all night. Mrs Drabble hath lost 10 cows of the cattle plague, a very fine day.

Saturday 27th.

Wm. fetched 4 score stakes and 3 bunches binding out of Northwood Car, then he went to Baslow Mill with 3 qrs. oats, went to the brickyard for 200 bricks to make 2 goose coats. Took the black horse to Chesterfield fair but did not sell him, a very fine day, Mrs Drabble hath lost 13 cows.

Sunday 28th.

I and Mrs Henry and Wm. White went to Darley Church in the morning, Mr Hall preached in the afernoon at Beeley.

Monday 29th.

I began building the gees coats, fetched Mr Sculthorpe one load of coals from Rowsley. Saw Mr Cottinham at night had some talk with him about takeing to Mr Jepsons post horses and the yard. Wm. began ploughing the far commonpiece. Mrs Drabble hath lost 15 cows and Mr Worrall condemned the others to death, 2 affected and 2 that is not affected with the disease, the Duke is to pay her for them that thay order slaughtered, a very fine day.

Tuesday 30th.

Wm. ploughing in the far common piece, I was building the gees coats in the morning. Wm. Lees and I went rabbiting in the afternoon caught 2 rabbits, Jacob Towndrow making edging stones for the garden in the afternoon in the burnt wood, Father looking after the cattle. Sold young shaw to go no Tuesday next to Mr Cawdwell of Winster, for 20£, a fine day some drisly rain at night.

Wedensday 30th.

[*Two 30ths in his diary, gone wrong somewhere*] Jacob Towndrow and I working in the garden all day. Wm. ploughing in the far common piece, Father looking after the cattle, a fine day.

Thursday 31st.

Thrashed some in the morning, Wm. ploughing the remainder of the day, a very dirty afternoon, working in the garden a wile then shaking some straw &e.

Friday 1st February.

Working in the garden a little, Jacob in all day. I went to Bakewell sent 40£ in half notes to Messrs Thorpe Newark, went to Baslow Mill in the afternoon for the 3qrs of oats, got something mended at the sadlers. Wm. ploughing a very fine day, Father looking after the cattle,

Saturday 2nd.

William fetched 2 loads of edging stones out of Rowsley Wood then he went ploughing the remainder of the day. He took one load of manure up with him, I and Jacob working in the garden and finished one of the gees coats, a fine day but roughf wind.

Sunday 3rd.

Very wet in the morning part, Mr Hall preached in the afternoon.

Monday 4th.

I went to Bakewell should have been the market day wanted to have bought a fat pig or two but did not hear of any except Mr Furniss of Longstone, thay have 3 feeding he promised me the chance of them when thay are fat. Sent the remaining half notes to Newark 40£ completed, sent half notes 15£ and Post Office order 1£10s. makeing when completed 16£ 10s. to J & C Sturge of Birmingham for Indian corn. Wrote to Mr Jackson of Hull and Mr Irving of Chesterfield for prices of Linseed cake. Jacob in the garden, Wm. took one load of manure up with him ploughing in the far piece. Sent an order to Newark for 10 sacks SSS flour 39s 4d. 10 sacks SS 37s.4d. 4 Sacks A 35s 4d. 20 cwt fourths 8s 6d. 20 cwt bran 4s 9d. A fine day. Mr Jepson sent me 2qrs of malt 60s. per qr. Bought some goosberries and 1 apple tree from S Mawrey of Thornbridge.

Tuesday 5th.

Mr Cawdwell came for the fat cow, we went to Mr Cottingham for a pass but he could not sign it, thay killed her at our place. Helped Jacob in the garden in the afternoon/ Wm. ploughing in the far piece, he took one load of manure with him, Father looking after the cattle. Sent half 5£ note to the paraffin light Compy. of Birmingham, a windy day some showers of rain.

Wedensday 7th.

[Note. *He appears to have been wrong with the dates since 30th January*] Thrashing in the morning whe thrashed all that is in the barn, only one stack out of doors. Wm. took one load of manure with him he was ploughing the remainder of the day. Jacob and I in the garden a little then whe set a troughf in the orchard for the ducks to drink out of. Cawdwell fetched the cow she weighed nearly 51 stones he paid for her, I trapped my finger very bad with seting the machine down, I sent off the remaining half notes ot Messrs Sturge of Birmingham, wrote a letter to Mr Travis sent him a newspaper yesterday. A very deal of rain fell this morning and a deal fell tonight, some storms during the day.

Thursday 8th.

I and Jacob working in the garden, Wm. ploughing in the far common piece, the first goose laid an egg, had 3 cwt. of carrots of Holmes of Matlock 3s. per cwt. A very fine day.

Friday 9th.

Winnowing 12½ qrs. of oats ridled some chaff for J Halksworth and Matt. Towndrow, sent an order for 2 tons

127

cake, sent the last half 5£ note to the Paraffin Comp. Sent Mr Mayhew 2 gals. Oil , a very wet day.

Saturday 10th.

A showy day I got the horses shod, took some things to be mended went to Darley Mill for 3 sacks flour and 12st. bean meal, took one paraffin cask to the station. All of us in the garden in the afternoon, Jacob ridled some chaff in the morning, Wm. lining up thatch in the morning.

Sunday 11th.

A very rainy day, found a year old calf in the Lydget nearly dead, Wm. went to Bakewell to Shenton he sent some medicine for the remainder. Whe skinned the calf in the afternoon, died of the speed.

Monday 12th.

I went to Rowsley for the cake that I had of Mr Jackson of Hull, Wm. fetched the calf from the Lydget that died yesterday. He went to Calver for chits in the afternoon for the garden walls, Jacob in the garden all day, I helped him in the afternoon. Father looking after the cattle, a fine day.

Shrove Tuesday 13th.

Wm. went to Shubley for coal for Mr Spencer and Mr Sculthorpe 1 ton each, got home soon after 1 o'clock, I helping Jacob in the garden, Cawdwell killed Buckleys cow at our house in the morning, a good deal of snow fell very fast last night, I went to the Hill Top to Mr H Lees at night.

Wedensday 14th.

Getting half of a stack of oats in in the morning then Wm. and Jacob getting manure out of the yard got about 14 loads in the Mains, Domney and G Buckley helped us to get the stack in. The snow wastes and some showers fell, Mr Worral went to the Lydget to set some soughing out, Father went to Bakewell to the board room.

Thursday 15th.

Wm. and I fetched 2100 two inch pipes from Rowsley brickyard and 350 4 inch pipes took them into the great Lydget except one load which is left till morning, took 3 horses in one cart from home. Jacob in the garden all day, a very fine day. Got an envoice from Newark of 26 bags flour 10 bags sharps and 10cwt. bran. Mr Holmes called to see us he stoped all night with us, I ordered 2 tons bone manure of him for sowing on grass land.

Friday 16th.

Wm and Father took one load of tiles to the Lydget then whe fetched the flour &e from the Station, allso 2 bags of bean meal that Mr Else had left at John Elliott for me. Whe thrashed about an hour, a very fine day, Jacob in the garden.

Saturday 17th.

Wm. took one load of manure in the far common piece then he was ploughing all day. I was jobing about in the morning, I went to Baslow in the afternoon for 3qrs. of oats, took Mr Mayhew some flour, got some harness

'I went to Baslow in the afternoon for 3 qrs of oats'
© Derbyshire County Council

mended at Mr Marples, Jacob in the garden all day, a fine day.

Sunday 18th.   Rather frosty.

Monday 19th.   Lead 12 loads of manure in the Mains, I built the end of the other goose coat up, fetched 2100 2 inch pipes and 600 3 inch pipes from Rowsley Brickyard in the afternoon. Jacob filling manure in the morning, split some stakes in the afternoon, a fine frosty day.

Tuesday 20th.   Took 2 loads of tiles to the Lydget, got 7 loads of manure on, lead 6 loads of stone for the drains that is to be made in the great Lydget. I set some goosberry trees in the garden, went to Rowsley for one load of coals for J Halksworth, a fine day. Drabble calved early this morning a red cow calf.

Wedensday 21st.   Took 2 loads of tiles to the Lydget, then Jacob I and Wm. leading stone to the drains, lead 22 loads. Killed Buckley's *a big space*, pig?, got a apple pit in. The Dukes soughfers began soughfing in the great Lydget, a very fine day, frosty until noon. Mr Buckley brought some fruit trees from Smiths of Darley, one Glant Morcean Pear planted at the bottom end of the old garden, one May Duke Cherry up the side of the old garden about 3 yards from the wall. One Victoria Plum at the end of the Kitchery, one Marie Louise Pear by the side of Ludlams House towards the other end, next a Victoria Plum by the wall at the other end of the garden. 2nd a red Orlean Plum, third a apple tree that I bought from Mr Mawreys at Thornbridge, fourth a Victoria Plum, 5th a Greengage Plum.

Thursday 22nd. Wm. and Jacob leading manure for Wm. White untill noon, the whe took a load of tiles with 2 horses, lead stone the remainder of the day. Jacob I and Father set the troughf and made the end of the soughf in the old lane. A very fine day, frosty in the morning, sent Miss Wheatley a green chee and a few apples in a hamper.

Friday 23rd. Thrashed about an hour in the morning, then Wm. fetched 2 loads of lime from Stoney Middleton. Jacob walling at the bottom end of the great Lydget in the old lane. Holmes of Matlock took 10 pks of apples paid me for them 1£. Smedley took 6 stones thay are to be 2s 6d. per stone. I went to Bakewell to a meeting of the Cattle Insurance Compy. very showery at times.

Saturday 24th. Took the lime in the great Lydget mixed some dirt out of the soughfs with it, took 2 stones to go over the troughf, Jacob walling Wm. and I breakng stone into the soughf the remainder of the day. A very fine day.

Sunday 25th. Went to Darley Church in the afternoon, a fine day. Roan neck calved a wite cow calf about midnight.

'Went to Darley Church in the afternoon'
© Derbyshire County Council

Monday 26th.	Wm. fetching soil and sand for the garden, I helped Jacob to wall a little at the bottom end of the Lydget, a fine day rather roughf morning.
Tuesday 27th.	Leading manure for Matth. Grindey in the forenoon with 2 horses, then Wm. fetched one load of edging stones out of Rowsley Wood, Jacob and I putting down edging stones and making the border. Paid Joseph Halksworth 5s for edging stones. Wm. and Jacob leading manure for John Halksworth with 2 horses in the afternoon, rather roughf some parts of the morning. The great roan 4 year old heifer calved a roan cow calf about 5 o'clock this morning.
Wedensday 28th.	Wm. took the black horse to Chesterfield Fair, I took the light cart and boxer, sold the black horse for 16£. Jacob sharpening stakes and ridling chaff. Father looking after the cattle, a very roughf frosty cold morning, snow allso.
Thursday 1st March.	I and Father went to G Wilsons sale, Wm. leading manure for T. Buckley. Jacob making edging stones for the garden walls and tieing up thatch, a very frosty fine day.
Friday 2nd.	Thrashed about an hour in the morning, lead 7 loads of manure in the mains, fetched 2 loads of wood from the Lees, allso the turnip drill whe brought home, Jacob set a few edging stones, frosty day.
Saturday 3rd.	Wm. fetched one load of sand to the cowhouse groop [*sic*]. John Downs took half the groop up and relaid it, Jacob and I helping him all day. Made a drain out of the cowhouse into the yard where the dung is laid. Wm. fetched Mr Sculthorpe 2 loads of manure from Rowsley, then he went to Rowsley Brickyard for 1200 3 inch tiles in the afternoon. The frost appears to be going. *Note: The groop, or group, was the area immediately behind the cows in the cowshed in which manure was deposited*
Sunday 4th.	I went to Darley Church in the morning, Father went to the Thornbridge, rather frosty. My niece Mary Ann Turner is staying a few days with us.
Monday 5th.	Gillett calved this morning a little wite cow calf. Wm. and I took 800 tiles to the Lydget with 2 horses, lead 4 loads of stone to the soughf. I went to Mr Wards sale at Matlock in the afternoon bought 1 drake and 2 ducks cost 16s. let Mr Holland have one duck 3s 4d. Wm. fetched one load of coal for Mr Sculthorpe, Jacob shaking straw and cleaning up in the morning, seting edging stones in the afternoon, a fine frosty day.
Tuesday 6th.	Wm. fetched Mr Sculthorpe 4 loads of coal and Miss Hawkins 1 load, took 2 qrs. of oats to Edenor Mill,

winnowed 6½ qrs of oats. Jacob ridled some chaff, he set some edging stones in the morning, a good deal of snow fell some melted as it came. Ellen and Elizabeth Milnes came, Buckleys children was here to tea allso.

Wedensday 7th.

A day of Humiliation and Prayer on account of the Cattle Plague. I found one ewe with her womb down she seems to be going on allright, a very fine day. I and G Wilson and T Buckley went to Darley Church at night.

Thursday 8th.

Took some stakes and bindings into the mortingreave, loaded 400 tiles to go to the Lydget, took 2 horses with them after dinner, loading stone the day out. Jacob did not

GOVERNMENT AND THE CATTLE PLAGUE.

THE cattle plague has now become a great fact, and a most distressing one. The reported cases from the commencement of the disease show that 132,183 animals have been attacked; that of these 17,368 have been killed; that 81,386 have died, and that only 16,055 have recovered. But this is unhappily under the truth. These returns are only derived from the information received at the Veterinary Department of the Privy Council office; many returns ought to have been added to these, but for the neglect of some of the inspectors; while there have doubtless been several cases of disease and death of which the inspectors throughout the country have not been informed. But this result in itself is sufficiently startling. Nor can we see any reason to believe that the disease is on the decrease; for though the number of animals attacked in the week ending February 3 was only 9,153, as compared with 11,745 in the previous week, if we compare that week with the one still preceding—i.e., ending January 27—we find that the number attacked was 10,041-; so that it would seem that the next return is just as likely to show an increase as a decrease.

Cattle plague
Bakewell Standard
24 Feb 1866

*Cattle plague
Bakewell Standard
24 Feb 1866*

> ## BAKEWELL.
>
> The following is a return of cattle lost in the Bakewell District by the cattle plague :—
>
> 26th January, Mrs. Drabble, Harwood Grange, 33 killed and buried. all badly affected.
>
> 22nd February, John Lee, farmer, Foolow, 9 killed, all badly affected.
>
> 24th February, Joseph Bottom, Great Longstone, 2 killed and buried, both badly affected.
>
> 26th February, John Archer, farmer, Meadow Place. 24 killed, some buried, some burnt ; 84 others, affected or not, but all ordered to be destroyed ; Thos. Potter, farmer, Curbar, 15 killed and buried, badly affected.
>
> 2nd March, Margaret Makisson, farmer, Priestcliffe, 12 killed and buried, badly affected.
>
> 3rd March, Edward Mycock, farmer, Flagg, lost 1, 3 other milk cows, badly affected, shot and buried.
>
> 5th March, Thos Wild. Foolow, 1 milk cow affected, shot and buried ; James Bagshaw, 1 milk cow affected, shot and buried.

come in the morning, breaking stone into the soughf after dinner, I was helping him. Fine day rather frosty.

Friday 9th.

Jacob Wm. and I breaking stone into the soughfs thay were at it all day. I went to Bakewell after dinner, fine day frosty, bought a pig of S Gardner last night 2£ 12s 6d.

Saturday 10th.

I and Jacob finished the wall across the old lane, pudled the soughf to bring the water into the troughf. Wm. leading stone with one horse all day. Father got the early potato put in. A very fine day but roughf wind, I gave the men that is draining 1 Gallon Ale.

Sunday 11th.

A fine day but windy.

Monday 12th.

Wm. finished ploughing the far common piece before dinner then he was leading stone after dinner to the drains, a very fine day.

Tuesday 13th.

Wm. went to Stoney Middleton for lime, Jacob breaking stone half of the day into the soughfs, spread some manure after dinner in the great Lydget. I went to Sheffield by the Coach, bought 10qrs. of black oats of Joshua Outham for seed at 25s 6d. per qr. Mr Furniss of Burchill is to have half of them, he bought 21qrs. of white ones at 30s per qr. in Redford. I am to have 5 qrs. of them. A very stormy day, allso very frosty, called at Storth House had some tea there, came by Coach from Owler Bar to Baslow.

Wedensday 14th.

Wm. leading stone, gathering tiles up &c. I mixed the 2 loads of lime with with some dirt and clay before dinner. Wm. and Jacob leading manure in the mains. Wm. went into Rowsley wood for edging stone at night, I went to Darley Mill brought 1 bag of bean meal paid for it, allso

'Wm. went to Stoney Middleton for lime'
© Derbyshire County Council

some bacon I had of Mr Else some time since, 3£ 17s 6d. Sent Messrs Thorpe 30£, the Paraffin Compy. 5£, sent 52 sacks to Newark 30 of mine and 22 of Thorpes. Sent an order for 10 qrs. of Indian corn to Messrs Sturge, Birmingham, sent an order to Newark for 12 sacks flour SSS, 8 sacks SS, and 4 sacks A, 20 cwt of bran and 15 or 20 cwt. of fourths, a very fine day but frosty.

Thursday 15th.

Wm. leading manure for Buckley's, I and Jacob making edging stones, weeling stone into the walk and breaking stone and seting edging stones, a dirty day, rather snowey at times.

Friday 16th.

Wm. leading manure for Thos. Wilson, Jacob at Thos. Wilsons. I was breaking stone and putting it into the soughf at Lydget, a very fine day, some of the men finished draining, Munks and Jim Downs hath not finished, took one drain into Henry Lees field to bring water across the top of the Great Lidget into the old lane. Artington calved at night, a wite cow calf.

Saturday 17th.

Wm. fetched 5 qrs. of wite oats from Hassop Station that I had of Mr Furniss costing 32s.per qr. including carriage, took 3 qrs. of oats to Edensor Mill, borrowed 1 sack of Indian Meal of Mr Mortimer. I finished making the walk in the garden. Jacob spreading manure in the mains most

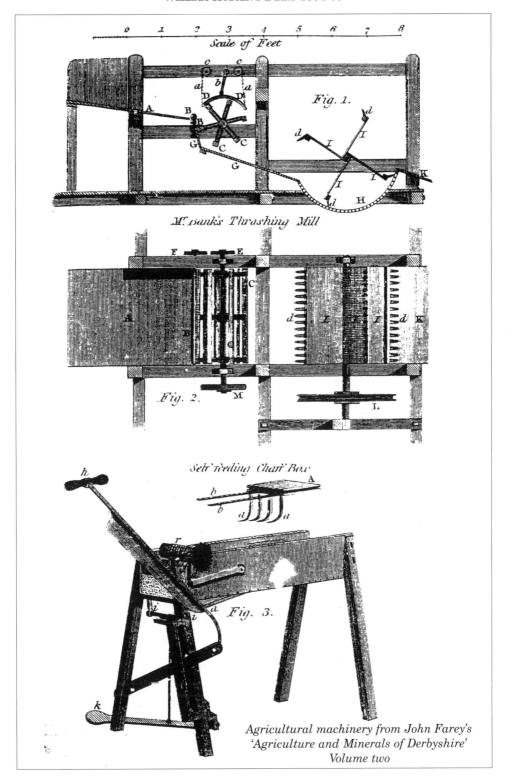

Agricultural machinery from John Farey's
'Agriculture and Minerals of Derbyshire'
Volume two

of the day. Whe finshed thrashing all the oats that is in the barn. Wm. and I went to Rowsley Station for 2 tons of bone manure, Rosy calved early this morning, a red bull calf. Filled up a paper with the average value of each of our cattle, the 8 milch cows I average at 16£ 5s each, the 6 2 year old at 10£ 3s 4d. each, the four year old at 5£ 5s. each, 6 young calves at 2£ each. Some rain fell during the day, it rained hard at night. Set both gees with 13 eggs each.

Sunday 18th. A fine day.

Monday 19th. Wm. leading stone from the top of the Park to the bottom of the Stand Wood for the Duke, Jacob spreading manure in the Mains. I went to Bakewell sold Henry Lees the 3qrs. of oats that went to Edensor Mill and Mr Briddon 4 qrs. of the same sort 11 stone 7lb. Gross at 28s. per qr. A fine day.

Tuesday 20th. Wm. leading stone for the Duke, he fetched 2 tons of Indian corn from Rowsley Station, Jacob did not come. I went to Mawreys sale at Thornbridge, the first ewe lambed 2 tup lambs, slight rain in the morning then fine but very cold.

Wedensday 21st. Wm. leading stone again, the ewe had her womb down again, I fomented and put it back and stitched her. Mr Furniss of Longstone called he bought the chees 35 in number at 75s per cwt. He bid money at 2 stirks 18£, I wanted 20£. I went to Henry Lees sale in the afternoon, a fine day but cold, I went to Ashford at night, stayed all night.

Thursday 22nd. Got home about half past 9 in the morning, the ewe lambed 2 lambs that had her womb down she is doing well. Wm. leading stone at Chatsworth, I was gardening some, set some cabbage plants and early potatose, 2 rows of peas, sowed some parsley seed and some radish seed, some snow in the morning but a fine day.

Friday 23rd. Wm. ploughing in the Bering gate in the forenoon with 2 horses and in the afternoon with one horse. I took the chees to Longstone after dinner 5 cwt. 1qr. 6lb. Received for the chees 19£ 17s. got the mare shod at Pilsley as I went, came back by Bakewell, bought ½ gallon of brandy with me. A very cold day, very cold and wet as I came home, Perishing allmost. I gave a hog that was scouring some laudnum in some salt and water at noon, tonight it died I think I gave it too strong a dose, bought 2 couple of fowls of John Turner at 5s. per couple.

Saturday 24th. Wm. leading stone at Chatsworth with 2 horses, I began pleaching a [h]edge between the Mortin Greave and Pits, it rained in the afternoon.

Stepping stones over the River Derwent near Beeley Bridge
© W. H. Brighouse

Sunday 25th.	A fine day, another sheep lambed one lamb.
Monday 26th.	Wm. took two loads of bones in the Mortin greave and pits, then he went ploughing the remainder of the day in the Bering gate. Jacob and I sowed 16 bags of disolved bones in the Pits and16 bags in the Martin greave, did a little pleaching a very fine day, another sheep lambed one lamb.
Tuesday 27th.	Wm. ploughing in the Bering gate, Jacob and I walling some gaps up on the bottom of the Pits, then whe did a little pleaching. I went as a bearer to John Holmes funeral, a fine day I fetched the Dukes chain harrows out of the Park.
Wedensday 28th.	Wm. chain harrowing in the Mortin greave and Pits and in the Mains, Jacob rooled the Mortin greave, I fetched 4 score stakes and 12 rails out of the Beeley plantation then whe finished pleaching the [h]edge between the Mortin greave and Pits.
Thursday 29th.	Jacob and Wm. getting manure out of the yard into the mains, I helped them fill a little, Killed a pig of our own took 4 qrs. of oats to Bakewell in the afternoon for Thos. Briddon he did not pay me for them. Jacob Wm. and

Father got the last oats stack in. I sent 20£ half notes to Thorpes of Newark, a fine day another sheep lambed one lamb.

Friday 30th. Good Friday Cut the pig up, 23 stones, took 5 sheep and 7 lambs in the bering gate to eat the rape off. Mr Vizitelly called to see us, a very fine day.

Saturday 31st. Whe thrashed some, winnowed 3 qrs. of oats. I took some flour for Halksworth at Lees,and Frank Hawley got Boxer shod, got a new set screw put in the pulley belonging to the thrashing machine. Mr Spencer paid me his bill, Mr Buckley paid me, Mr Marsden paid me 3£ on acct. 2 sheep lambed 3 lambs making 10 lambs of 7 sheep, a good deal of rain today, agreed to let Thos. Froggatt have 1 ton of seed hay at 5£ per ton, he fetched 4 trusses towards the ton.

Sunday 1st April. A fine day, 2 sheep lambed 3 lambs one died. I went to Mr Mayhews.

Monday 2nd. Jacob spreading manure in the mains, Wm. got the straw that went out with the manure together. 2 sheep lambed 4 lambs, Father and I went to Bakewell Market, or rather should have been the Easter Fair. Paid Mr Holmes of King Sterndale for 2 tons of bones disolved, I ordered some clover seed of him. Paid Mr Else 25£ 17s. ordered some flour and one side of bacon at 9d. per lb. Very wet in the afternoon some snow.

Tuesday 3rd. Wm. went to Boythorpe for 2 tons of coal for Mr Spencer, Jaccob and I in the garden, finished laying the flags at the front door and made a larder. Went to a vestry meeting at night, rather finer. John Oxspring called I sold him a barren ewe for 3£ a very small one.

Wedensday 4th. Wm. leading stone to the highways with 2 horses, I went to Joseph Lees bought 7 pigs of him very good ones at 63s. each, sent Thorpes the last half 20£. I went to Ashford in the afternoon brought a drink for Rosy, she is not well, a fine day.

Thursday 5th. Wm. leading stone to the highways, I killed another pig, Jobing about home sowed another row of peas and one of beans. Trussed Thos. Froggatt 8cwt 2 qrs. and 1lb of hay. Rather snowy at times. Father went for Shenton to come to Rosy but he was not at home

Friday 6th. Wm. and I fetched 12 sacks flour and 15 of offals from Rowsley Station, then Wm. fetched one load of nut slack from P Bailey. He led some manure out of the yard after dinner. 5 more sheep had 5 lambs yesterday and today. Mr Potter came and I sold him 9 hoggs at 55s. each. Shenton

*Guide stoop on Beeley Moor pointing out the old road from
Chatsworth to Chesterfield*

© H. Smith

called and looked at the cow that is not well, she is rather better, a very cold day rain at times.

Saturday 7th.   I went to Chesterfield Fair rode back with Mr Hopkinson, Wm. rowling the mains, Jacob seting quicks between the Mortingreave and pits, a very cold day. Paid Joseph Lees for the pigs.

Sunday 8th.   A fine day.

Monday 9th.   I was jobing about all day, went to Edensor for a pass to move some sheep Mr Potter bought. Mr Wain came sold him 3 stirks for 30£ to go this day fortnight, Mr Furniss called, Jacob in the Mains seting quicks, a fine day. Wm.went to Owler Bar for 5qrs. of black oats I bought of Joshua Outham.

Tuesday 10th.

Wm. leading stone to the Highways, Jacob seting quicks in the Mains, I set another row of peas and one of beans, made the bed for the shalots and set them, a drizzly day Father helping me.

Wedensday 11th.

Jacob I and Wm. about home, some rain during the day, made a thatch stack spun some ropes to truss hay with, lead some manure in the afternoon. Wm. took some tiles to the Lidget and harrowing in the far common piece.

Thursday 12th.

Wm. leading manure for Thos. Wilson, Jacob spreading lime in the lidget, trussed Thos Froggatt some hay, fetched 30 buckett full of swill, a deal of rain last night.

Friday 13th.

Jacob I and Wm. sowed about 4 acres in the far common piece, I went to Bakewell in the afternoon. Killed J Halksworth a pig, Ann Hibbs took 2 pigs for D Milnes and brought 2 fat ones from Furniss's of Longstone, the 1 weighed 13 stone 1 lb, the other 14 stone. I paid her 2s. for fetching them, Mr Potter paid the remainder for the hoggs.

Saturday 14th.

Sowed the remainder of the far common piece Jacob I and Wm., a very heavy day, a fine day too.

Sunday 15th.

A Fine day.

Monday 16th.

Sowed the South field, Thos. Froggatt sent us a man and horse. Sowed the oats that came from Redford there and about 2 pecks of peas. A very fine day but roughf wind.

Tuesday 17th.

Wm. ploughing in the hiring gate, Jacob and Father getting potatose in, I helping them a little. Fine day but roughf wind, sowed the onions.

Wedensday 18th.

Sowed half of the bering gate with black oats, then I gardened some. Jacob diging in the garden then harrowing in the afternoon.

Thursday 19th.

Wm. ploughing in the hiring gate, Jacob seting potatose in the garden, sowed the carrots and another onion bed, some early potatose is coming up, a very fine day.

Friday 20th.

Wm. ploughing in the hiring gate he finished it. I went to Bakewell got a certivicat signed to move 3 stirks. Jacobs helping Wm to finish the headlands, a very fine hot day.

Saturday 21st.

Whe finished sowing oats in the bering gate, Mr Wain fetched 1 ton of hay. Whe ridled 3½ qrs of hay seeds, an uncommon hot day. Had a fat pig of Mr Worral on Thursday.

Sunday 22nd.

A very hot day.

Monday 23rd.	Ridled another qr. of hayseeds sowed them and the small seed in the bering gate. Wm. sowed the hay seeds and Jacob rowled the south field in the forenoon. Jacob led some manure in the Mains in the afternoon, Wm. rowled the hiring gate. I went to Woodthorpe and stayed there all night, paid Josh. Outham for 5 qr black oats, Mother came to Beeley, a very fine day.
Tuesday 24th.	Wm. making the potato ground ready in the far common piece, Jacob rowled the oats. I went to Sheffield, bought a heifer of Brother George, paid him for her 13£, he is to have the calf.
Wedensday 25th.	Wm. took one load of manure to the far piece and 2 trusses of hay for the calves, then he began crosscuting the fallow in the wood close. Jacob fiinished the old garden seting, he and I went 'edging between the pits and the Mortin greave.
Thursday 26th.	Wm. ploughing Jacob 'edging, then whe cleaned up the refuse where whe pleached, spun some ropes, a fine day.
Friday 27th.	Wm. ploughing, whe trussed 1 ton of hay for Mr Furniss of Baslow. Jacob spread some manure in the Mains, then he gathered some stones after dinner. Mr Furniss's man came for the hay in the afternoon. Father, Henry and George went to meet Brother George for the heifer I bought of him, thay met George at the top of Ramsley, a very hot day some thunder.
Saturday 28th.	Wm. finished cross cuting the fallow then whe fetched 3 loads of flour &e from Rowsley Station. I ran the manure over with the chain harrow in the mains, fine day but cooler. Lent John Holmes the harrow, he broke one piece in it, I broke another.
Sunday 29th.	A very fine day.
Monday 30th.	Wm. began breaking down the fallow, I went to Bakewell Market, got too much to drink, sold Mr Furniss some hams at 1s per lb. A dry day.
Tuesday 1st May.	Wm. in the fallow, I gardened some, a very hot day.
Wedensday 2nd.	Wm. in the fallow, slight showers of rain.
Thursday 3rd.	Wm. in the fallow, I gardened some, showers of rain.
Friday 4th.	Wm. in the fallow he had only one horse in the afternoon, I took one to Ashford and Longstone, took Mr Furniss 11 hams, 247lbs at 1s. per lb A very fine day
Saturday 5th.	I and Wm. rowling and chain harrowing in the Great Lidget. Wm. fetched some Indian meal from the Mill. I sent George and Henry to the Storth House to tell Brother George to fetch the calf off the heifer that I bought off him,

she calved this morning a cow calf, a dry day.

Sunday 6th.	I and Wm. Downs went to Darley Church in the morning, a fine day.
Monday 7th.	Brother came for the calf, Henry and George came with him, thay got here at half past 7 in the morning. I and Father Henry and Wm. went seting potatose in the far common piece, a fine day.
Tuesday 8th.	Whe were seting potatose all day, finished seting. I went to Graftons at night, cut his pigs he paid me his bill.
Wedensday 9th.	Wm. went to the Lidget gathering stones and spreading dirt out of the soughs that the men had left in heaps. I went to Pilsley got the cart mended and some irons made to put the wire neting round the garden, some rain.
Thursday 10th.	I put some wire up by the garden, Wm. and Father and Henry gathering stones in the lidget, a good deal of rain last night.

In Beeley Village
© Julie Bunting

EDENSOR
DEATH OF MR. WILLIAM HODKIN

We regret to announce the death of Mr William Hodkin, Bridge House, Edensor, which took place last Friday, after an illness extending over some weeks. The deceased was one of the best known men in the district. He took an active part in public matters up to quite recently. A farmer and miller in an extensive way of business, he found time to devote to public matters. As a Guardian he paid close attention to the interests of the parish, and as a Parish Councillor his advice was always valued. He was 69 years of age, and leaves a widow and 5 sons to mourn the loss of one of the best of husbands and most considerate of fathers.

The funeral took place at Beeley Parish Church, on Monday, and was very largely attended by relatives and friends. The service was conducted by the Rev. H.C. Sculthorpe (vicar), assisted by by the Rev. J. Hall (vicar of Edensor). The coffin, which was covered with a number of beautiful floral tributes, was of English oak, with brass furniture, and on the plate was the inscription:—

WILLIAM HODKIN,
Died July 28th, 1899,
Aged 69.

The bearers were Messrs. F. Dakin, D. Bailey, S. Booker, S. Holtham, J. Stone, E. Morton, E. Holmes, E. Fern, G. Hulley, and J. Clay. The principal mourners were Mrs. Hodkin (the widow), Mr. and Mrs. H. Hodkin (Manchester), Mr. and Mrs. Charles Hodkin, Mr. and Mrs. George Hodkin and family (Beeley), Mr. and Mrs Chas. Hodkin and family (London), Mr and Mrs. Horace Hodkin (Wellingborough), and Mr John Hodkin Beeley.

Amongst other relatives and friends also present were Mr. and Mrs. Hutchinson (Fulwood), Mr. and Mrs. Siddall (Dore), Mrs. George Hodkin (Totley), Miss Bower and Miss Nichols (Calthorpe), Mr. and Mrs. Spitalhurst (Hope), Mrs. Skidmore (Calton House), Mrs. Bramwell (Stockport), Miss Mary

Fisher, Mr. Cheeseman, Mr. Gasper, Mr. Turnbull, Mr Turner (Chatsworth), Mr. Hearnshaw (Edensor), Mr. J. Hodgkinson (Matlock) Mr. Dickenson (Rowsley), Mrs. Harrison (Edensor), Mr. A. J. Adams, Mr. A. Plant, Mr. C. Critchlow (Bakewell), Mr. Newbold (Buxton), Mr. Carline (Beeley), Mr. Anderson (Rowsley), Mr. and Mrs. Morton (Beeley), Mr. Wardley (Bradford), Mrs. Dakin (Youlgreave), Mr. and Mrs. Ben Stone (Beeley), Mrs. Clay (Fallinge), Mrs. Buckley and Mrs Doxey (Beeley).

With acknowledgement to The High Peak News, Saturday 5th, August 1899.

EDENSOR.
DEATH OF MR. WILLIAM HODKIN.

We regret to announce the death of Mr. William Hodkin, Bridge House, Edensor, which took place last Friday, after an illness extending over some weeks. The deceased was one of the best known and most respected men in the district. He took an active part in public matters up to quite recently. A farmer and miller in an extensive way of business, he found time to devote to public matters. As a Guardian he paid close attention to the interests of the parish, and as a Parish Councillor his advice was always valued. He was 69 years of age, and leaves a widow and five sons to mourn the loss of one of the best of husbands and most considerate of fathers.

The funeral tok place at Beeley Parish Church, on Monday, and was very largely attended by relatives and friends. The service was conducted by the Rev. H. C. Sculthorpe (vicar), assisted by the Rev. J. Hall (vicar of Edensor). The coffin, which was covered with a number of beautiful floral tributes, was of English oak, with brass furniture, and on the plate was the inscription :—

WILLIAM HODKIN,
Died July 28th, 1899,
Aged 69.

The bearers were Messrs. F. Dakin, D. Bailey, S. Booker, S. Holtham, J. Stone, E. Morton, E. Holmes, E. Fern, G. Hulley, and J. Clay. The principal mourners were Mrs. Hodkin (the widow), Mr. and Mrs. H. Hodkin (Manchester), Mr. and Mrs. Charles Hodkin, Mr. and Mrs. George Hodkin and family (Beeley), Mr. and Mrs. Chas. Hodkin and family (London), Mr. and Mrs. Horace Hodkin (Wellingborough), and Mr. John Hodkin (Beeley).

Amongst other relatives and friends also present were Mr. and Mrs. Hutchinson (Fulwood), Mr. and Mrs. Siddall (Dore), Mrs. George Hodkin (Totley), Miss Bower and Miss Nicholls (Calthorpe), Mr. and Mrs. Spitalhurst (Hope), Mrs. Skidmore (Calton House), Mrs. Bramwell (Stockport), Miss Mary Fisher, Mr. Cheeseman, Mr. Gasper, Mr. Turnbull, Mr. Turner (Chatsworth), Mr. Hearnshaw (Edensor), Mr. J. Hodgkinson (Matlock), Mr. Dickenson (Rowsley), Mrs. Harrison (Edensor), Mr. A. J. Adams, Mr. A. Plant, Mr. C. Critchlow (Bakewell), Mr. Newbold (Buxton), Mr. Carline (Beeley), Mr. Anderson (Rowsley), Mr. and Mrs. Morgan (Beeley), Mr. Wardley (Bradford), Mrs. Dakin (Youlgreave), Mr. and Mrs. Ben Stone (Beeley), Mrs. Clay (Fallinge), Mrs. Buckley and Mrs. Doxey (Beeley).

Obituary of William Hodkin as it appeared in the High Peak News 5 August 1899